C0-BWY-055

FLORIDA STATE
UNIVERSITY LIBRARIES

MAR 8 1995

.TALLAHASSEE, FLORIDA

The
Urban
West

THE URBAN WEST

Managing Growth and Decline

JAMES B. WEATHERBY
AND
STEPHANIE L. WITT

PRAEGER

Westport, Connecticut
London

HT
384
U5
W43
1994

Library of Congress Cataloging-in-Publication Data

Weatherby, James Benjamin.
    The urban West : managing growth and decline / James B. Weatherby
and Stephanie L. Witt.
        p.   cm.
    Includes bibliographical references and index.
    ISBN 0–275–93998–7 (alk. paper)
    1. Cities and towns—West (U.S.)—Growth.   2. Urban policy—West
(U.S.)   I. Witt, Stephanie L.   II. Title.
HT384.U5W43   1994
307.76'0978—dc20   93–43062

British Library Cataloguing in Publication Data is available.

Copyright © 1994 by James B. Weatherby and Stephanie L. Witt

All rights reserved. No portion of this book may be
reproduced, by any process or technique, without the
express written consent of the publisher.

Library of Congress Catalog Card Number: 93–43062
ISBN: 0–275–93998–7

First published in 1994

Praeger Publishers, 88 Post Road West, Westport, CT 06881
An imprint of Greenwood Publishing Group, Inc.

Printed in the United States of America

∞™

The paper used in this book complies with the
Permanent Paper Standard issued by the National
Information Standards Organization (Z39.48–1984).

10 9 8 7 6 5 4 3 2 1

To

Dana Lynn Weatherby

and the memory of
Donna Rae Crawford Witt
1932–1992

Contents

Tables and Figures

TABLES

FIGURES

Acknowledgments

We are grateful for the support and encouragement of a great number of people who helped make this book possible.

First of all, we would like to thank Boise State University for providing financial support for this undertaking, and former President John Keiser, whose vision of an urban university's commitment to public affairs helped inspire this work. We would like to also thank Dean Robert Sims, who has encouraged us all along the way and helped provide the idea for our title, *The Urban West*.

There are several students who have provided significant assistance. We are particularly indebted to Lorna Jorgensen, who played a key editorial role during the latter stages of this project. Other students who provided assistance include BethAnn Skamser and Mollie Creswell.

Our colleagues in the Public Affairs Program and in the Political Science Department at Boise State University are a never-ending source of wit and wisdom. We especially thank Rebecca Meyer and Tricia Trofast, office coordinators, and W. David Patton for his help in the preparation of the tables and figures.

Professors David J. Olson of the University of Washington and Nicholas Lovrich of Washington State University read early drafts and provided invaluable insights and suggestions.

We would be remiss if we did not express our gratitude to many unnamed colleagues who had special knowledge of our ten Urban West focus cities. They serve in offices of state municipal leagues, city halls, chambers of commerce, state departments, daily newspapers, and other places throughout the Urban West. They were invaluable in providing insights and guiding us to key information and people.

Most important, we want to thank those who mean the most to us and who have endured our anxieties and frustration throughout the too-long period in which this book was taking shape. Dana Lynn Weatherby played a crucial role. She was a constant source of support, encouragement, and wise counsel. John and Maran Weatherby, who will one day write their own books, were and are always a source of inspiration. Ben and Jean Weatherby contributed much in their own special way. Friends like Leslie Stubbs, Linda James, Kym Dye, Peggy Guiles, Sue McCorkle, Meghan Watters, and Rebecca Scott formed a support system that made finishing the book possible. To all of these we gratefully acknowledge our thanks.

1

Introduction

This book is a study of the limitations imposed on cities and their struggle to implement policies and maintain services during a decade (1978–1988) of rapid growth in the West. Unlike their Grecian ancestors, they are not city-states. Like American cities generally, western cities are important partners in our American intergovernmental system, but they do not have inherent powers of local self-government. They are, in Paul Peterson's (1981) terminology, "limited cities." All American cities operate within an environment of limits. They are limited in a formal, legal sense because they derive most of their powers from law or constitution. As the phrase goes, they are creatures of the state. Cities are limited by their economic context. They are small pawns in a larger national, even global economy. Decisions made in corporate board rooms, far removed from city boundaries, often have more impact on communities than do the actions of their elected officials. It would seem, then, that western cities' struggle toward local autonomy and economic self-sufficiency would be doomed. No amount of home rule authority or economic development will give them absolute independence. In spite of this situation, cities fight against their limits, asserting the value of local initiatives and local discretion. The fight for greater local autonomy "has been a century-long struggle and an article of faith among local officials" (Wright, 1988:312).

Urban West cities have struggled against their limits in recent years either to promote growth or to respond to growth's impact on municipal services and facilities. The population and economic growth in the Urban West have focused attention on cities and their ability to serve both new and existing residents. They have raised questions about how much growth is beneficial, who should pay for growth, and how growth can be managed. Reactions to growth have raised further questions about the meaning of local autonomy, the power of elected officials to implement their policies, and the rights of citizens through the initiative and referendum process to restrain or modify local policies.

CITIES AS LIMITED ACTORS

An important theoretical contribution to our understanding of urban politics and the role of cities in growth-related policies is embodied in Paul Peterson's (1981) book, *City Limits*. Peterson contends that to understand the behavior of cities, urban scholars need to shift their focus from the internal politics of cities to the "external" constraints of economic forces largely shaping urban policy making. With the exception of allocation policies, Peterson's "economic constraint" model gives little credence to the impact of political forces or, as he calls them, noneconomic factors. In other words, in most major municipal decisions, the need for communities to grow economically and to expand their tax base is far more influential in the decision-making process than such noneconomic factors as the type of governmental structure, the degree of neighborhood activism, or the nature of mayor-council interactions. According to Peterson,

> because cities have limits, one explains urban public policy by looking at the place of the city in the larger socioeconomic and political context. The place of the city within the larger political economy of the nation fundamentally affects the policy choices that cities make. In making these decisions, cities select those policies which are in the interests of the city, taken as a whole. It is these city interests, not the internal struggles for power within cities, that limit city policies and condition what local governments do. (p. 4)

Peterson also asserts that city politics are "limited politics" in part because of the constraints that the U.S. federal system places on local government. He argues that to try to understand the behavior of cities without understanding their limited powers within our federal system is to overlook critical considerations. The impact of our federal system is seen in the rise of federal mandates on cities and congressional preemption of municipal authority during this period. These mandates include new federal laws and regulations requiring cities to improve their air and water quality, limit the use of tax-exempt municipal bonds, and participate in the Social Security system. The federal courts also imposed significant restrictions, particularly in the areas of limiting municipal bond authority and requiring municipal compliance with federal employment legislation (Fair Labor Standards Act).

Although it has not been widely discussed in the theoretical literature, the limits placed on cities by state government are extremely significant. There is very little that cities do that is not mandated or authorized by the state government through statute or constitutional provision. These state provisions include such constraints on city governments as specifying the form of government, determining how cities are financed, and limiting the extent of their regulatory powers. In addition, the actions of other local governmental entities have some impact on city prerogatives. Local school districts or highway districts, for example, that can implement their own public facilities plans without city input can have a major impact on city service and growth patterns.

A city's interest, in Peterson's argument, can be summarized as those actions that enhance the city's economic health, social prestige, or political power. He states that there is a "unitary interest" within the community to support economic growth. The sometimes negative effects of growth, such as neighborhood congestion and dislocation, are seen as less significant than the need to promote the wealth of the community, which is seen as a benefit to all stakeholders in the municipality. Peterson further argues that it is the fiscal capacity of the community that determines its expenditures on various services rather than either genuine demand or the effects of internal politics.

Thus, the major limits within which a city must operate include its own fiscal capacity and whatever constraints might be imposed by other levels and units of government. Peterson explains the importance of these environmental variables by demonstrating that city spending on welfare as well as redistribution policies are largely unrelated to the need for those policies (i.e., the presence of poor citizens), but rather reflect the economic capability (i.e., per capita income) of the city to provide the redistribution service.

Peterson's work spawned a series of studies defending and criticizing his economics-driven model of city behavior. Judd and Kantor (1992) summarized the evolution of the study of urban politics since the publication of Peterson's 1981 book:

City politics has come to be understood as a continuous, complex interaction between politics and private institutions, between the marketplace and the public sphere, between private goals and collective purposes. The scholarship that is devoted to the study of these interactions has been labelled the "political economy" approach, which we believe encompasses most, though certainly not all, of the research on urban politics today. (p. 1)

Many scholars have questioned the extent to which city choices are indeed "limited" in the way Peterson suggests. Even though their perspectives vary on municipal political economy issues, Swanstrom (1989) and Wong (1988) raise questions about the heavy emphasis on economic market in Peterson's analysis. Swanstrom argues that Peterson overstates the extent to which economics controls city decision making, and he takes note of the many instances in which local political forces have come to dominate a city's political agenda. Wong argues that studies of new policy adoption, structured reform, service delivery, neighborhood organizations, and taxpayer revolts "can serve as useful supplements" to Peterson's economic constraint model (p. 5). It is apparent to Wong that "institutional practices" and "political influence" have more of an impact on policy adoption and implementation than Peterson suggests (p. 23).

This more balanced approach to the role of politics and economics is evident as well in the "urban regime" literature. Judd and Kantor refer to the urban regime approach as one that includes an analysis of the "tensions between local democracy and the marketplace" (pp. 4–5). This urban regime, initially presented by Elkin (1992), is also used by Stone (1992), who defines an urban regime as "the informal arrangements by which public bodies and private interests function together in order to be able to make and carry out governing decisions" (p. 51). The result of Peterson's work and the development of the political economy and urban regime approaches to urban politics has been a recognition that legal limitations and external economic forces are critical elements in understanding city decision making. A focus solely on the internal politics of cities or solely on the economic constraints of cities is incomplete.

The extent to which cities are in fact limited to following an economic logic and to which issues are decided by political forces will no doubt differ from city to city, and will likely change within individual cities over time. The following discussions draw on an approach to urban politics that recognizes both the impact of constraints on cities and the degree to which city officials, operating within these constraints, can influence the quantity and quality of growth within their boundaries.

Further constraints are placed on cities by their own citizens, often acting either to restrict taxing powers, as in property tax revolt–like measures, or to slow up or even stop growth as seen in our case study of citizen-initiated growth controls in Modesto, California. The increasing use of these direct democracy tools raises a question about the distinction between local autonomy and democracy (Conroy, 1990). Local control has generally meant that local officials had the ultimate say on issues that directly affected communities. Today, the concept is a bit more complex, as citizens increasingly use the initiative process to affect city policy. Who should prevail in matters of local control: the electorate through the direct democratic process (initiative, referendum, and recall) or the community's elected representatives?

Each chapter begins and ends with this theme of limited cities and how they have developed and implemented policies either to respond to or to encourage growth in their communities.

UNIQUE INFLUENCES OF THE WESTERN POLITICAL CULTURE

The title of our book, *The Urban West*, may seem to some to be a strange oxymoron. The West, known for its big-sky country, wide-open spaces, and frontier, is rarely viewed as a region of significant urban places. In fact, however, some of its states are among the most urbanized in the country. Utah and Nevada are as urban as New York and Massachusetts. Best known in the West are the largest cities: Los Angeles, San Francisco, Denver, Phoenix, and Seattle. Much has been written about them. But there are a significant number of cities, thirty-four, in fact, that range in population from 100,000 to 200,000. (For a complete list, see Table 2.5.) These cities, as limited actors, are the cast of characters for this book.

The Urban West cities are of medium size, but they are real cities with many of the same major urban problems and service-delivery issues faced by our nation's largest central cities. They are not merely bedroom communities whose existence is totally dominated by and dependent on a much larger central city. No one family or industry dominates their existence, but they are not large enough to avoid taking huge hits when major industries leave. They are big enough to play significant roles in enhancing the quality of life of their citizenry but not so large that they cannot be affected by direct action of ordinary citizens through initiatives, recalls, neighborhood protests, and so forth. They have the resources and capacity—professional and financial—to become major participants in the development of this country.

In many respects, the West is a unique region. A comparative study of Western cities would be incomplete without at least a brief understanding of the historic and political context in which these cities operate. The influences of municipal reform, property tax revolts, and public lands are more predominant in the West than in any other part of the country (see Thomas, 1991). Municipal reform proposals had a major impact on the West, even though some of these states were not in existence during much of the early days of the reform movement. Western cities typically use many reform features, such as council-manager forms of government, nonpartisan elections, at-large council seats, and initiative and referendum processes.

The property tax revolt that started in California in 1978 made a deep impact on the West, spreading to Nevada and Idaho, and subsequently to Colorado and Oregon. The property tax revolt would not have gotten off the ground in the West without the prevalence of such direct democratic devices as the initiative and referendum. These tools of direct democracy are used in the West not only for property tax-protest purposes but also for growth management. Growth management was a predominant issue during the decade of our study, 1978–1988, because the West was growing—more rapidly, in many respects, than any other region of the country. With growth came conflict over its benefits and power struggles in many communities over how much growth should be tolerated.

Underlying this property tax aversion, however, is the typical Western hostility toward government. "Complaints of 'big government' and 'high taxes' strike a responsive chord among self-reliant Westerners," according to Scott Mackey (1991:2) of the National Conference of State Legislatures. Mackey has noted the Western ability to export their tax burdens to other parts of the country through natural resource charges on hydroelectric, mining, timber, oil, and gas industries. This tax-avoidance mentality helps explain why three out of the five states in the country that do not have sales taxes are in the West—Alaska, Montana, and Oregon—and six of the nine states without personal income taxes are in the West—Alaska, Nevada, South Dakota, Texas, Washington, and Wyoming (Mackey, 1991). It should not be surprising, then, to find that many of the state and local tax structures in the West are not particularly well balanced. They typically rely heavily on only one or two major revenue sources. The 1990 tax revolt in Oregon can be attributed to the state's almost 50 percent reliance on one revenue source, the property tax. California in 1978 mirrored Oregon, with almost the same percentage property tax burden. Most of the other states in the Urban West face similar tax problems because of unbalanced tax structures, with the exception of Idaho and Utah (Snell, 1990).

Another important limitation on municipal government, and another reason for such a high incidence of tax revolt activity in the West, is the widespread use of the initiative process. Almost every Western state gives its citizens direct lawmaking authority through a petition and initiative method. This gives angry citizens and taxpayers a "handle" to grab hold of government when they think it is out of control or has gone too far in its taxation decisions. It was through this process that the tax revolt began in the West in 1978, and it was also through this process that a 1.5 percent property tax-limitation initiative passed in Oregon in

1990. According to David Magleby (1988), the decade of the 1980s saw major increases in the use of statewide initiatives.

Other parts of the country, notably Massachusetts, have suffered from the geographic spread of the property tax revolt, but its serious impacts have been primarily in the West. California, Nevada, and Oregon have been especially affected, and Idaho—even with a relatively balanced tax structure—has also been hard hit by the tax revolt.

The West has also been deeply affected by the presence of the federal government, which owns huge amounts of land. This has made the federal government, even though an important factor in the development of the West, a hated absentee landlord in the latter part of this century. When Westerners attack government, in most cases they are really complaining about the federal government.

Yet another Western characteristic is the heavy emphasis on the benefits of economic development. Economic-development concerns have dominated Western thinking and policy making. One of the reasons for this emphasis, as noted by Thomas, is the lack of economic diversification and Western reliance on outside interests.

Western leaders are concerned about their dependence on natural resources, agriculture, and government, and the fact that world prices and decisions in Washington often determine the economic well-being of the West. This has led to a search for economic diversification and independence in order to insulate the Western states from these external influences (Thomas, 1991:13–14).

THE URBAN WEST STUDY

We wrote this book because of our fascination with city government and our belief that cities are important and interesting in and of themselves. We have spent most of our professional lives either studying urban government and politics or working directly on the challenges that beset municipal governments.

When we refer to cities, we primarily mean municipal governments. City governments are our central unit of analysis, and our focus is primarily on the public sector. Other actors in this study are typically viewed from the perspective of cities. When we speak of partnerships with the private sector or the work of other groups, it is from the perspective of city government. We believe that every one of our Urban West cities has the potential to avoid the mistakes of our country's largest cities, to overcome the intractable problems that beset most of the nation, and to shape future courses in ways that would maintain human scale in the midst of growing metropolises.

This book is for both practitioners and students of urban government. We deal with "real-world" issues as well as the factors explaining the underlying patterns and diversities found among Western cities. Two bodies of excellent work inform this analysis: One is rooted in the theoretical and empirical work of political science and economics, the other in public administration. The first body of literature addresses abstract questions such as how the city should be governed, the proper relationships in American federalism, and the theoretical relationships between economic policies and city welfare. The second takes up the applied questions of what cities are actually doing and how they can be made to operate more efficiently and democratically.

Students of urban politics are enriched by having exposure to both literatures. It is critical to have some sense of the larger picture and to develop a framework to understand the political and economic forces shaping urban politics. It is also imperative to understand the major concerns of the people who actually run our cities and to have some sense of how they go about their jobs. In this book we hope to do both.

The Urban West study was formed out of an interest to find the common issues and challenges facing medium-sized cities in the West. Most scholarly and popular attention has focused on the nation's largest cities, particularly on the East Coast and in the Midwest. As mentioned earlier, the attention that has been given to Western cities is primarily focused on the region's largest cities, such as Seattle, Portland, Denver, Los Angeles, and San Francisco. The focus of this comparative study, however, is on the medium-sized cities (100,000–200,000 in population), many of which still have time to avoid the mistakes of their larger and better-known neighbors.

We have chosen to focus primarily on a decade of cities' experience. Our decade begins in 1978 because of the impact the property tax revolt had on cities. In addition, 1978 marked the beginning of a period of substantial cuts in federal aid to cities.

Our study is based on information and data gathered about all of the cities in the population range of 100,000 to 200,000 in eight Western states: Arizona, California, Colorado, Idaho, Nevada, Oregon, Utah, and Washington (cities in this population range comprise the thirty-four Urban West cities). In addition, we present more in-depth information from a core group of ten "focus cities": Tempe, Arizona; Modesto, California; Pueblo, Colorado; Boise, Idaho; Reno, Nevada; Salem and Eugene, Oregon; Salt Lake City, Utah; and Tacoma and Spokane, Washington.

These focus cities were chosen because of their population range, their status as "second-tier" cities in the West, and because they view or have viewed each other as economic development competitors (Mabbutt and Lyman, 1985:18). Additional reasons for these focus cities' selection include the following. Initially, an important factor was that we are located in the City of Boise. We began our comparative analysis with a view to studying cities that were fairly comparable to Boise. All of the focus cities generally meet this criterion. Our view also coincided with an earlier study done by the Boise Future Foundation (Mabbutt and Lyman), which had studied the revenue and expenditure patterns of the same cities. According to the foundation study, the "sister cities" were selected because of their "population size, demographic composition, proximity to Boise, and frequency with which such cities are mentioned as alternative sites for business or residential location" (Mabbutt and Lyman, pp. 18–19). In addition to these considerations, we were also interested in these cities for their similarities and differences. We wanted to look at their reliance on the property tax, their growth-management strategies, and their successes in promoting economic diversification.

The information used in this book is based on census data, information gained from interviews conducted with city and community leaders in each of the focus cities, and documents and reports obtained from the cities. In selecting people to interview, an effort was made in each city to achieve a balance between city officials and representatives of the general public. The city officials typically included city administrators, finance staff, and one or more elected officials. We also drew upon private-sector resources, ranging from local media representatives, business leaders, and other interested citizens. In some states, information from state highway departments was utilized. Many state municipal leagues and county associations have participated in our interviewing and information gathering as well. The expertise of state municipal league staff was utilized in almost every state in which our focus cities are located. They helped provide an informed outsiders' perspective, recognizing that a key responsibility of the staff representing cities in any state is to have their finger on the pulse of their state's cities. They were useful in furnishing compilations of reports that helped provide some context for the role of our focus cities in the state's legal and political environment. They were also helpful in recommending knowledgeable people who could offer valuable interviews.

Finally, where appropriate, we have relied on data from the Advisory Commission on Intergovernmental Relations and on information from the International City Management Association's *Municipal Yearbook* series.

In the following chapters we will focus on cities that have dealt with some of the challenges of growth and the reality of their own limitations. Chapter 2 focuses on the impacts of state and federal government policies and actions on cities, and the degree to which citizens, through the initiative process, have limited city government options in financing and growth management in a number of Urban West cities. Chapter 3 discusses city officials' attitudes toward growth and how municipal growth management measures can be imposed by state legislation or citizen initiative. The discussion in chapter 4 focuses on the decline in the quality of municipal infrastructure and the funding limitations and growth pressures that lead cities to shortchange their spending on infrastructure. Chapter 5 is concerned with alternative revenue sources for infrastructure and other city services. The move away from the heavy reliance on the property tax and the creation of other financing mechanisms for growth-impacted public facilities and services are analyzed. Chapter 6 discusses how cities are driven to implement aggressive economic development policies. It describes the public-private partnership cities have entered into to achieve their economic development goals.

2

1978–1988: A Decade of Change for Cities in the West

Growth in its many dimensions was the issue of our Urban West decade of 1978–1988. Municipal powers and responsibilities were substantially changed to address growth in property taxes, growth in national governmental intervention in municipal affairs, and growth in population within many cities. Some of these changes arose as citizen-led initiative campaigns successfully limited municipal government's most important source of local revenue—the property tax. Other changes arose from ideologically driven policy proposals, ostensibly designed to reverse the increasing centralization of governmental power in Washington. These efforts included the national government's defining cities' responsibility for programmatic and financial policy making in several domestic policy areas: the environment, communications, personnel, finance, and so forth. This important shift in policy implementation was accompanied by the withdrawal or decline of federal funding for many established urban programs. As noted in chapter 1, many cities in the Urban West faced rapid population growth, increasing the numbers of citizens demanding services at the very time that resources for meeting those demands were diminishing. Local initiative efforts in the West addressed population-growth issues with the passage of measures intended to manage and control the explosive growth in some Western cities. For Paul

Peterson's limited city (1981), this period of time presented enormous challenges.

This chapter will examine how those challenges have been addressed in the Urban West by explaining the role of cities in our federal system; changes in federal funding affecting cities; the impact of the property tax revolt on Urban West cities; and the population growth experienced by the region.

FEDERALISM AND CITIES

As suggested earlier, cities must be analyzed within the constraints that our federal system places upon them. Federalism is a system of powers divided between a national government and subnational governments; in the United States this entails the national government and the fifty state governments. The powers and responsibilities of the national and state governments were originally set forth in the Constitution of 1789. Much of our nation's history can be understood as an evolution of the relationships between the several states and the national government. Cities were not key players throughout most of this history. As a telling fact, it should be noted that cities were not even mentioned in the Constitution. Municipalities and other units of local government were originally, and largely remain today, subservient to their state governments; until the 1930s they had very little direct contact with the national government, either financially or programmatically.

Of all of the units of local government, however, cities generally have enjoyed the most autonomy and flexibility. Most county governments, except for those that are large and urban, are essentially administrative arms of state government. Much of what they do is mandated by state law, and their daily activities typically involve administering statewide programs. Similarly, school districts are closely governed by state law and often are guided a great deal by a state department of education's policies and regulations. Other local government entities such as special districts and township governments have limited functions and limited revenue sources with which to carry out their functions.

Despite their relative degree of autonomy, cities—like other units of local government—are almost wholly dependent on their state governments. Their discretionary powers, such as they are, can be significantly limited by state action at any time. They typically have to look to the state laws or constitution to find the authority to engage in a particular function or service (Rhyne, 1980). The U.S. Advisory Commission on Intergovernmental Relations (ACIR) has undertaken many studies of the problems and issues surrounding state-local relations and the degree of autonomy enjoyed by local units of government. In early 1982, the ACIR undertook a comprehensive analysis of the local discretionary authority of cities and counties in the United States. Key factors used to rank these local governments included financial powers, flexibility in structuring their governments, personnel administration, and control over the services they provided and functions they performed in each of these areas. This study ranked discretionary authority among cities and counties throughout the country. Cities in the Western states ranked near the bottom, especially those in Colorado, Nevada, and Idaho. (See Table 2.1 for ACIR's ranking of local discretionary authority.) Oregon cities and counties had the most local discretionary authority among Urban West cities, and Idaho cities and counties had the least.

Dillon's Rule limits local discretionary authority in most states. Dillon's Rule derives its name from the Iowa State Supreme Court Justice who wrote the opinion in a case relating to municipal powers. Judge Dillon ruled that cities are creatures of the state and that they possess no implied powers beyond those specifically accorded them by their state (*City of Clinton v. Cedar Rapids and Missouri River Railroad Co.*, 1868).

Consequently, when assessing the range of policy choices a city might have, it is necessary to look at the constraints state laws and constitutions have placed on a particular city. The influence of Dillon's Rule calls attention to the external environment of the city and city efforts to mitigate the impact of Dillon's Rule. One of the most significant efforts has been to authorize, through a constitutional or statutory amendment, home-rule powers for cities.

Most home-rule provisions authorize cities, either by statute or constitutional amendment, to engage in functions and services not in conflict or denied by state laws or constitution, or to specify certain functions and services as being "municipal affairs" over which cities should be given broad discretion. The first type of authorization is known as the "residual powers" home rule. This approach is designed to overturn Dillon's Rule. The basic intent is to give cities authority to engage in local functions and services that are not denied to them by either the state constitution or state law, rather than allowing them to operate only under specific legislative grants of authority that are unambiguously given.

The other type of home rule is called the *imperio in imperium* approach, in which cities are given broad grants of authority in "municipal affairs" that are not of statewide concern and should not be mandated or controlled by the state legislature. This situation is not unlike the dual federalism of the nineteenth century, in which states attempted to carve out functions and services that were exclusively of a statewide concern, beyond the control of the national government. Cities have used home-rule charters in an attempt to create spheres of influence that are primarily matters of municipal concern, not subject to state legislative interference. These spheres include such things as governmental structure, types and

Table 2.1
States Ranked by Degree of Local Discretionary Authority, 1988

	Composite (all types of local units)	Cities only	Counties only
1.	Oregon	Texas	Oregon
2.	Maine	Maine	Alaska
3.	North Carolina	Michigan	North Carolina
4.	Connecticut	Connecticut	Pennsylvania
5.	Alaska	North Carolina	Delaware
6.	Maryland	Oregon	Arkansas
7.	Pennsylvania	Maryland	South Carolina
8.	Virginia	Missouri	Louisiana
9.	Delaware	Virginia	Maryland
10.	Louisiana	Illinois	Utah
11.	Texas	Ohio	Kansas
12.	Illinois	Oklahoma	Minnesota
13.	Oklahoma	Alaska	Virginia
14.	Kansas	Arizona	Florida
15.	South Carolina	Kansas	Wisconsin
16.	Michigan	Louisiana	Kentucky
17.	Minnesota	California	California
18.	California	Georgia	Montana
19.	Missouri	Minnesota	Illinois
20.	Utah	Pennsylvania	Maine
21.	Arkansas	South Carolina	North Dakota
22.	New Hampshire	Wisconsin	Hawaii
23.	Wisconsin	Alabama	New Mexico
24.	North Dakota	Nebraska	Indiana
25.	Arizona	North Dakota	New York

levels of services, municipal boundary issues (including annexation), and local taxation. Two areas of particular relevance are the annexation and taxation powers of cities. Of the ten Urban West focus cities, only Tempe and Pueblo exercise home-rule authority and have certain unique powers granted in their charters that are not available to other cities operating under the general laws of their respective states. This is particularly the case with regard to their ability to impose alternative forms of local taxes (Charter for the City of Pueblo, Colorado, 1983; Charter for the City of Tempe, Arizona, 1984).

Home-rule powers are important for cities, especially in granting them the authority to determine their own funding sources and service levels

Table 2.1 (continued)

	Composite (all types of local units)	Cities only	Counties only
26.	Florida	Delaware	Wyoming
27.	Ohio	New Hampshire	Oklahoma
28.	Alabama	Utah	Michigan
29.	Kentucky	Wyoming	Washington
30.	Georgia	Florida	Iowa
31.	Montana	Mississippi	New Jersey
32.	Washington	Tennessee	Georgia
33.	Wyoming	Washington	Nevada
34.	Tennessee	Arkansas	Tennessee
35.	New York	New Jersey	Mississippi
36.	New Jersey	Kentucky	New Hampshire
37.	Indiana	Colorado	Alabama
38.	Rhode Island	Montana	Arizona
39.	Vermont	Iowa	South Dakota
40.	Hawaii	Indiana	West Virginia
41.	Nebraska	Massachusetts	Nebraska
42.	Colorado	Rhode Island	Ohio
43.	Massachusetts	South Dakota	Texas
44.	Iowa	New York	Idaho
45.	Mississippi	Nevada	Colorado
46.	Nevada	West Virginia	Vermont
47.	South Dakota	Idaho	Missouri
48.	New Mexico	Vermont	Massachusetts
49.	West Virginia	New Mexico	--
50.	Idaho	--	--

Source: From State and Local Holes in the Federal System (p. 262) by the U. S. Advisory Commission on Intergovernmental Relations, 1982, Washington, D.C.: Author.

as well as in designing governmental structures that will meet the unique needs of their communities. It also frees them from always seeking state legislative authorization for every new policy or program they are considering adopting and implementing.

Home rule is not the panacea that early reformers envisioned, however (Colman, 1975; Rhyne, 1980). One of the real barriers has been the difficulty in distinguishing strictly local functions from state functions: "The concepts are unclear, largely because of the shifting responsibilities of state and local government in a rapidly changing, complex society. . . . What is clearly a local function in one era may become clearly a state function in another" (Weatherby, 1978:20).

Even though they have been reluctant to make such distinctions, the courts "have interpreted narrowly the scope of powers granted to the local units" (Zimmerman, 1992:169). Where there is no judicial controversy, cities are constrained by state legislative actions. For example, while Tempe and Pueblo both heavily utilize local option taxation authority under their charters, they are still constrained by state limits imposed on revenue and expenditure levels.

The role of cities in our federal system changed with the economic emergencies experienced by the nation in the 1930s. As a part of its relief and recovery efforts, the national government channeled federal assistance to many of America's largest cities. The opening of this direct relationship between the national government and cities became part of what is now called cooperative federalism—federalism in which there was increasing interdependence and sharing among all levels of government (Elazar, 1984). Since the beginning of this cooperative era in federalism, cities have become significant players in the intergovernmental system. It was during the early 1930s that a national organization representing city mayors was born—the U.S. Conference of Mayors (Healy, 1974). At the same time, another important organization, the American Municipal Association (later the National League of Cities), changed much of its focus from a professional reform organization to a lobbying organization committed to affecting national domestic policy (Healy, 1974). Prior to the late 1970s, these organizations succeeded in lobbying for more funding for cities. From 1962 to 1978, the ratio of federal aid to cities' *own source revenue* grew from 5 percent to 26 percent (see Table 2.2). However, with the reductions in federal assistance brought about during both the Carter and Reagan years, that ratio declined 11 percentage points—from 26 percent to only 15 percent by 1984 (Wright, 1988).

Urban West cities are typical of American cities that affiliate with one or both of these national municipal organizations. Some cities such as Pueblo, have gone a step further to hire their own lobbyists to represent them in Washington, D.C. Boise has budgeted funds for federal lobbying purposes.

Changes in Federal Funding

There are a number of reasons for cities to have technical assistance and even lobbying help in working with the many federal agencies and programs that affect them. The most important of these effects tends to be fiscal in nature.

The national government has supplied significant funds to cities, both by paying for part or all of major programs and through a system of grants-in-aid that transfers revenue to cities for specified purposes.

Table 2.2
Ratio of "Federal IGR" to "Own Source Revenue," All Western Cities, 1977–1990

	1977	1978	1979	1980	1981	1982	1983	1984	1985	1986	1987	1988	1989	1990
AZ	28	39	37	35	31	22	20	17	14	14	10	09	12	10
CA	17	19	20	20	17	14	13	10	10	07	05	04	04	03
CO	19	21	20	16	15	12	09	08	07	07	05	04	03	05
ID	42	47	42	32	39	25	25	19	20	20	13	07	12	14
MT	28	28	27	27	21	18	07	08	13	14	07	04	04	02
NV	14	24	26	17	08	14	15	06	12	14	11	07	07	05
NM	53	55	31	30	30	25	19	08	15	16	09	07	09	12
OR	31	39	36	32	26	18	16	19	15	13	08	08	07	05
UT	21	25	16	18	15	13	15	16	14	10	08	10	06	05
WA	30	30	31	27	24	20	13	10	10	08	07	03	04	04
WY	21	47	37	31	39	42	28	24	18	16	12	12	17	08

Source: U.S. Bureau of the Census, selected years.

There are various types of grants, but they generally fall under three primary headings: categorical grants, block grants, and revenue sharing.

Categorical grants are for very specific purposes, and they usually require the recipient to match some of the funds. Some of the current categorical grant programs were established during the Johnson administration. Categorical grants give a high amount of control to the national government, which determines the specific uses for which the money is allowed, and the least amount of discretion is given to local officials on using the money. Examples of these types of grants include programs for the interstate highway system and construction of waste-water treatment plants.

Block grants are the result of the consolidation of several categorical grants into one package, giving local officials more control over the specific projects on which they will spend the money. Block grants were instituted by the Nixon administration as part of its New Federalism concept. The intent was to begin giving more discretionary power back to state and local governments. Block grants fund such functions as community development, transportation, training, and so on.

The final form of federal grant assistance is revenue sharing. This involves directly returning federal money to localities, allowing them virtually full discretion in how the money will be spent. General revenue sharing (GRS) is an example of this type of grant. Ironically, GRS was born and died under presidential administrations that called their domestic policies "New Federalism." GRS began under Richard Nixon in 1972 and was terminated in 1986 during the Reagan presidency.

New Federalism

The emerging federal government–city relationship has not been without controversy. Federal assistance has been sought and defended by cities and their lobbyists. However, this close fiscal relationship has brought with it some clear negatives to cities, which value whatever limited autonomy they might possess. The national government's fiscal capacity to share money with cities has also allowed it to mandate how cities must act in carrying out certain national policies. With the federal dollars came "strings" that limited local discretion, reflecting the long-term trend in this country since the 1930s toward increasing centralization of power and responsibility at the national government level.

This trend was challenged by the New Federalism of the Reagan administration. When Reagan entered office in 1981, he revived a concept first adopted by the Nixon administration more than a decade earlier— New Federalism. The discussion of either Nixon's or Reagan's New Federalism here focuses on intergovernmental relations and the impact such policies had on cities. It is beyond the scope of our study to explore the

partisan and ideological motivations underlying each new federalism—
Nixon's interest in redirecting domestic policy away from Great Society
programs or Reagan's interest in reducing the federal budget and cutting
back on national governmental programs and authority. In simple terms,
New Federalism involves trying to return power and responsibility to
state and local government whenever possible. It is based on the ideological belief that the national government has overgrown its proper size
and overstepped its proper boundaries by interfering with decisions ly-
ing properly in the domain of state and local governments. There are,
however, significant differences between the New Federalism of Richard
Nixon and Ronald Reagan. Nixon seemed to be more concerned about
the devolution of national powers to states and localities. Reagan's New
Federalism embodied the rhetoric of devolution but focused more on
cutting the federal budget and reducing the size of the national government than reallocating governmental powers (Bowman and Kearney,
1993).

Federal interference is alleged to have been inherent in the system of
grants given by the national government to states and localities that
strictly limited what the money was to be spent on, as well as in the
growing body of federal regulations that applied to states and localities.
Wright (1988:53–54) has identified four "D's" that describe components
of the New Federalism: "deregulation (eliminating rules and regulations), devolution (delegating discretion to states and localities), . . . dec-
rementalism (budget cuts and major reductions in federal aid) [and]
decongestion (a major sorting out of responsibilities among the three
levels of government)."

Several of these components were embedded in a 1982 New Federalism proposal offered by Reagan that involved a massive "swap and turnback" of federal programs. The swap included having the federal
government assume full responsibility for Medicaid, and having the
states assume full responsibility for Aid to Families with Dependent
Children (AFDC) and food stamps. Medicaid and AFDC are structured
so that costs are shared between the states and federal governments,
while food stamps are funded entirely by the federal government. The
turnback involved "phasing out approximately forty federal education,
transportation, community development, and social service programs"
(Wright, 1988:55). This proposal, in its entirety, would have "drastically
altered the composition of nearly 75 percent of federal aid" (p. 56). Reagan's proposal was never enacted as proposed, but in its first several
years, the Reagan administration did initiate substantial changes in the
types and amounts of federal funds made available to state and local
governments.

The New Federalism of the Reagan administration placed new financial and programmatic responsibilities on cities, which may be more

properly called "shift and shaft federalism" (Gold and Ritchie, 1992:23). During the last ten years, many major federal aid programs for cities have been reduced or eliminated, and the growth in other programs has been severely limited. That's the "shaft" in Gold and Ritchie's characterization. The "shift" refers to the number of mandates that continue to be required of cities and other local units of government in a host of areas ranging from environmental protection to corrections. General revenue sharing, which had been supported as a program that gave at least token reimbursement to cities for some of these mandates, died under the Reagan administration because Congress did not like the "no-strings" aspect of the program and because of the need to cut spending and reduce the federal budget deficit. In short, revenue sharing was a misnomer. There was no revenue to share.

The death of GRS has had two important negative effects on many cities. GRS had provided funds to many cities that otherwise did not have federal funding, and it enhanced the capacity of cities to deal with their problems because of the discretionary authority granted. According to Anton (1989:69), GRS "may have been one of the most profoundly significant public actions in our history."

In terms of dollar amounts, GRS provided "more than one-fifth of all federal funds received by city governments" (D. Peterson, 1988: 21). The effects of the loss were clearly felt in cities that had budgeted these dollars for operating or ongoing expenditures (Steel, Lovrich, and Soden, 1989).

A recent study documented the effect of revenue sharing's loss on New England cities, a majority of which utilized GRS for ongoing expenditures. The findings were that these cities would have to increase taxes or reduce service levels to offset the lost revenue (Thai and Sullivan, 1989). Boise, having committed much of its GRS funds for police and fire department salaries, was hurt by the loss. The city did not have the revenue flexibility of cities in other parts of the country that allows them to increase taxes to make up for the losses (as will be seen later in Figure 2.4). At bottom, GRS provided something that other federal programs did not—a virtual "no strings attached" approach that allowed cities to use funds for their own priorities as opposed to those of the national government.

Other federal programs benefiting cities were hard hit during the Reagan years. Frank Shafroth (1989) of the National League of Cities (NLC) comments that during the 1978–1988 decade, urban programs were reduced by over 50 percent. (See Figure 2.1 for an illustration of how federal funding to all Urban West cities have declined in real dollars.) NLC's complaint was that the partnership that had been established in the early 1930s and reaffirmed during most presidential administrations had been dissolved under Reagan's New Federalism. Shafroth noted that the na-

Figure 2.1
Trends in Federal Intergovernmental Revenue for All Western Cities, 1977–1990

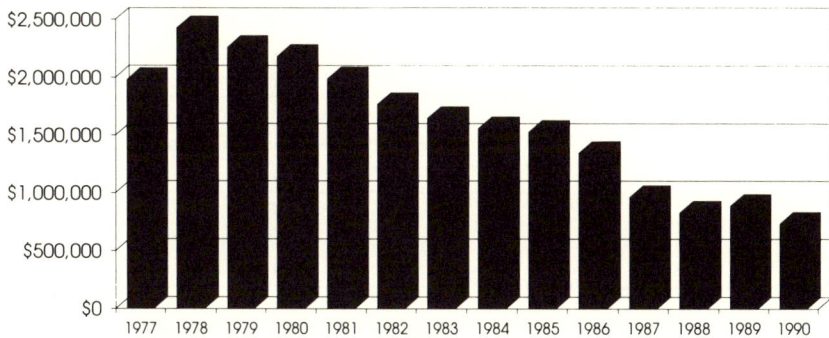

Source: U.S. Bureau of the Census, selected years.

tional government was giving more economic aid to two foreign coun-tries, Israel and Egypt, than to all of America's cities. As well, cities were beginning to be treated as representatives of just another interest group seeking a federal handout rather than as a partner in the delivery of important public services.

A report from the U.S. Conference of Mayors (1990) documented that from fiscal year 1981 to the proposed fiscal year 1991, federal funding declined by 70 percent for water purification projects, 59 percent for em-ployment and training, 54 percent for mass transit, 53 percent for com-munity development block grants, and 100 percent for urban development action grants—and, of course, revenue sharing was elimi-nated. To examine the impact of federal aid to cities, Bureau of the Cen-sus data were analyzed for the thirty-four Urban West cities. Using adjusted 1982–1984 dollars, Table 2.3 shows that per capita federal aid declined sharply from $88.59 in 1977 to $26.00 in 1987. As the national government's budget deficit grows more and more unmanageable, fur-ther roll-backs in federal support to cities can be expected.

During the decade of 1978–1988, cities were adversely affected not only by dramatic changes in fiscal federalism, but also by the imposition of stringent, locally initiated revenue or expenditure limitations. Dis-cussed in the following section are the various types of state-specific limits that often constrain municipal budgeting.

LOCAL TAX LIMITATION MEASURES

This section focuses on changes in local taxation powers that largely arose during the decade of 1978–1988. One cannot understand city pol-

Table 2.3
Selected Per Capita Revenue Sources for Thirty-Four Urban West Cities

Year	Federal Aid Per Capita[1]	Property Taxes Per Capita[1]
1977	88.59	107.99
1982	49.34	77.04
1987	26.00	106.98

[1]Adjusted real dollars.

Source: U.S. Census of Government Reports.

icies or the challenges city officials faced during this decade without appreciating the property tax limits under which cities struggled. Local tax limitation measures take many forms. Several are related to the property tax, which is the chief source of revenue for most local governments. The property tax is a tax on the value of property such as land and any improvements built on the land, like a house or a commercial facility. The assessed value of the property is determined by a local government assessor, usually a county officer. The property tax paid depends on the value of the property and the property tax rate set by the local government (e.g., city, county, school district, etc.). Property tax rates are expressed in mills, which is the thousandth part of a dollar, or sometimes in a percentage. For example, if a house was assessed at $100,000 and the property tax rate was ten mills (or 1 percent), then the property tax bill would be $1,000.

Limitations on the property tax can be placed on any of its three components: the assessed value of the property, the tax rate (mill levy), or the amount of revenue generated. Sometimes local tax-limitation measures combine limits on two or more of the above. California's Proposition 13, which passed in 1978, for example, has both a rate limit and assessment limit component. There are also spending limits that can be placed on the expenditures of a local government, or measures that require the government to publicize its taxation actions, called full disclosure limits. Each of these limitations is described in more detail below.

All of the above provisions are used in the Urban West states. In comparing local tax-limitation measures among the Urban West states, it is important to note that each limitation has certain provisions that allow some degree of flexibility in the setting of local levies. For example, most limitations provide a safety valve feature that allows a local government to exceed a limitation, subject to voter approval. There are also exemptions for such items as levies for bonded indebtedness, emergencies created by natural disasters, and other municipal obligations that are not considered to be part of a city's operating budget.

Property Tax Limitations

Rate Limitations. Rate limitations set maximum tax rates (mills or dollars per assessed valuation) that local governments can impose. Rate limits are in effect in Washington, California, Utah, and Idaho. There are two types of rate limits, general and specific. General rate limits apply to most, if not all, the local government property tax levies within a defined area, typically within a county. Specific limits apply only to particular types of local governments (city, county, special district, etc.) or to specific local functions such as police and fire protection or libraries (Gold and Fabricius, 1989). An example of how a rate limit affects the amount of revenue generated from property taxes is shown in Figure 2.2.

Revenue Limitations. These limits control annual increases in local property revenues. Arizona, Colorado, Nevada, and Washington cities have such restrictions. Idaho's revenue-limitation law was repealed, effective in 1992, by the legislature; Oregon's limit was replaced by a more stringent 1.5 percent rate limitation (Measure 5), passed by the voters in 1990. A property tax revenue limitation is illustrated in Figure 2.2.

Assessment Limitations. Assessment limitations are used in Arizona and California to control the annual increases in assessed valuation. Such limitations help reinforce and supplement rate limitations. In California, for example, under Proposition 13, annual increases in assessed valuation for properties that have not been sold within a tax year are limited to 2 percent. An example of an assessment limitation is included in Figure 2.2.

Other Local Tax Limitations

Spending limitations refer to percentage caps on annual local spending increases. Spending limits are used in both California and Arizona. For example, Arizona state law limits local expenditures to the base fiscal year of 1979–1980 with annual adjustments for increases in population, inflation, and city size (Morrison Institute for Public Policy, 1990).

Full disclosure, or "truth in taxation," provisions require local governments to advertise in paid notices when they are planning to raise property taxes. A public hearing is also mandatory. Utah adopted this

Figure 2.2
Property Tax Limitations

1. The City's Estimated Budget Needs (Spending) = Estimated Revenues (Budget Must Balance)
2. What Portion of Needed Revenues Come From Property Taxes?
3. Total City Property Tax Revenues (PTB) = Total Assessed Value of Property (AV) X Property Tax Rate (TR)
    PTB = (AV)(TR) To Figure the Tax Rate Solve For 'TR', TR = PTB/AV

Example One: Figuring the Property Tax Rate

Assume: City Assessed Value = $10,000,000.00
Needed Property Taxes = $150,000.00

X T.R. = Property Tax Portion of Budget - 150,000.00

TR = $150,000.00/$10,000,000.00
Tax Rate = .015 (1.5%)

$10,000,000.00

Example Two: The Property Tax With a Rate Limit of 1%

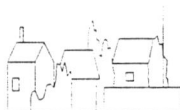

X 1% Fixed Rate = $100,000.00 available from property taxes for budget. If estimated portion of budget from property taxes was $150,000.00, as in example one, city must cut $50,000.00 worth of spending, raise other taxes or a combination of the two.

$10,000,000.00

Example Three: The Property Tax With a Revenue Limitation of 5%

IF: Last year's property tax revenue = $150,000.00, then the maximum revenue from property taxes allowed this year is $157,500.00 (a 5% increase).

X 1.575% (.01575) Tax Rate = 157,500.00 Portion of Budget From Property Tax
City A.V. = $10,000,000.00 (Assessed Valuation Stays the Same)

$10,000,000.00

X 1.5% (.015) Tax Rate = 157,500.00 Portion of Budget From Property Tax
City A.V. = $10,500,000.00 (Assessed Valuation Goes Up 5%)

$10,500,000.00

Note that the tax rate will go down as assessed valuation goes up when revenues are fixed as in this example.

provision in 1986. Idaho implemented its truth-in-taxation provisions during the 1992 tax year.

An understanding of some of the basic elements in the levy rate-setting process is useful in illustrating the operation of these various tax-limitation measures. (Included in this section are hypothetical illustrations of how these limitations would apply to a city government's budgeting process; see also Figure 2.2.) One of the first steps in the process is for locally elected officials to adopt a budget that includes all of their jurisdiction's anticipated revenue sources, including property taxes. The amount of the property tax portion of the municipal budget divided by the city's assessed valuation yields a city tax rate. The property tax rate-setting process can be expressed as $TR = PTB/AV$ where TR is the tax rate, PTB is the property tax portion of the budget (or that portion of property taxes subject to the limitation) and AV is the entity's assessed valuation for taxation purposes. For illustration purposes, visualize a city with a current assessed valuation of $10,000,000, a property tax budget of $100,000 and a levy of 0.01 (or 1%). If city officials decided that they needed to generate an additional $10,000 in property taxes for the next fiscal year, and they anticipated their new assessed valuation would increase by 10 percent to $11 million, their new property tax budget would increase by $10,000 with no increase in their current tax rate of 1 percent. However, if city officials decided they needed more property taxes, they could, depending on the type of limitation they were operating under, increase their levy to 1.5 percent and generate an additional $65,000 in property tax dollars from their increased tax base.

As noted in the prior discussion, most local budgets are not set in a vacuum. Property tax-limitation measures affect most budget-setting decisions. For example, a rate limit could mandate, as it does in California, that local levies cannot exceed 1 percent of assessed valuation, regardless of the growth in tax base or increased municipal costs. A revenue limit would allow an increase in property tax dollars only up to a fixed percentage, such as 5 percent. That would mean in our hypothetical case that the local officials could increase the property tax portion of their budget by no more than $5,000, rather than up to $10,000, an amount a city could levy if it had no such revenue limit.

Assessment limitations cap annual valuation increases by a certain percentage, such as the 2 percent ceiling in California. In our hypothetical case, the city's valuation will substantially increase over the current year's valuation of $10 million. But under an assessment limit such as California's 2 percent lid, its assessed valuation could only increase by $200,000, instead of $1 million; in other words, it could increase to a total of $9,200,000 rather than $10,000,000. If local officials were operating under a 1 percent rate limit in our example, they would only be able to increase taxes by $2,000, as opposed to $10,000 under the 1 percent and no assessment limits scenario.

Property Tax Revolt Begins in the West

Our history is strewn with tax revolts of varying intensity. Americans do not like to pay taxes and typically consider most taxes "too high" regardless of the criteria that are used to judge tax fairness. They especially do not like property taxes, as they have demonstrated in repeated opinion polls. The U.S. Advisory Commission on Intergovernmental Relations (ACIR, 1991) report, *Changing Public Attitudes on Government and Taxes*, reveals that the local property tax has often received primary attention as the worst and least fair tax.

In looking at a regional breakout of responses to this question (see Table 2.4), it is clear that in both 1977 and 1978, Westerners rated the property tax as the worst tax by some of the highest percentages ever recorded by the ACIR in its survey work spanning the period 1972 to 1991. In 1977, 45 percent of the Western respondents believed that the property tax was the worst tax; in 1978, 44 percent believed it to be the worst tax. These high numbers were only exceeded by the 54 percent in the West in 1972 who said they most hated the property tax. Other regions of the country in 1978 did not show the kind of disdain the West had toward the property tax. The percentage of respondents who ranked the property tax as being the least fair were as follows: Northeast region, 27 percent; North-central region, 35 percent; Southern region, 27 percent (ACIR, 1991).

This animosity toward the property tax can be explained in part by the confusion the general public has about the complexities of the property tax process, the lack of credibility in the administration of the tax, and the belief that the tax supports many services that do not benefit the property owner. Diane Paul (cited in Lowery, 1985) may have offered the best reason for the deep-seated emotional response to the tax. She argued that since people's homes are the object of the tax, they deeply fear the potential of losing their homes if they cannot pay the tax.

Given public attitudes toward the property tax, it should not be surprising that cities in each state in the Urban West have been affected by property tax-limitation measures such as rate or levy limitations enacted during the era of the property tax revolt, or limitations put in place in the decade or two prior to the revolt. Rate limitations were imposed in California, Idaho, and Nevada. Earlier rate limits were in place in Oregon, Utah, Washington, Colorado, and Arizona.

Clearly, local governments in these Western states are operating under severe fiscal limitations. All eight of the states involved in this study have property tax limitations—either limitations on rate, revenue, or assess-

Table 2.4
Which Do You Think Is the Worst Tax—That is, the Least Fair? Western Region, 1972–1991

	Federal Income Tax	State Income Tax	State Sales Tax	Local Property Tax	Don't Know/No Answer
1991	28	8	24	25	16
1990	Different Version Asked				
1989	28	11	19	23	19
1988	39	9	19	18	15
1987	28	10	20	28	14
1986	44	9	16	22	9
1985	39	13	17	18	13
1984	44	12	14	20	10
1983	43	8	14	21	14
1982	34	12	24	22	8
1981	40	8	14	30	9
1980	37	9	19	25	10
1979	45	9	11	24	11
1978	23	11	19	44	5
1977	25	7	15	45	7
1976	Question Not Asked				
1975	31	12	23	27	10
1974	29	4	19	38	11
1973	35	8	13	36	8
1972	18	12	11	54	5

Note: All numbers are percentages.

Source: From Changing Public Attitudes on Government and Taxes (p. 6) by the U. S. Advisory Commission on Intergovernmental Relations, 1991, Washington, D.C.: Author.

Figure 2.3
**Local Property Taxes as a Percentage of Total Local Tax Collections by State,
1977–1987**

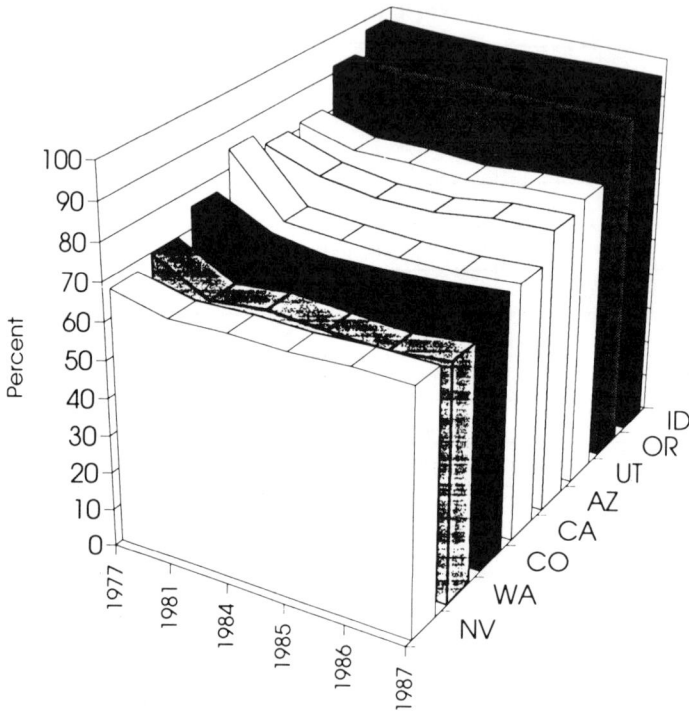

ment increases. Others of the eight states studied also have spending limitations on local governments (California and Arizona).

The impact of these various tax and revenue limitations on local governments can be displayed graphically. Figure 2.3, derived from data from the ACIR's (1987) report, *Significant Features of Fiscal Federalism*, displays the percentage of local tax collections in each of the Urban West states that were from property taxes in the period between 1977 to 1987. As Figure 2.3 indicates, several of the Urban West states have had a dramatic decline in the percentage of local tax collections based on the property tax. California's local governments experienced the greatest drop in the percentage of revenue derived from property taxes, falling from 85.2 percent of all local tax collections in 1977 (one year before Proposition 13) to 68.8 percent in 1987.

Washington, Colorado, Arizona, and Nevada, meanwhile, had an average decline of 5.3 percent in the percentage of local tax collections derived from the property tax in the decade between 1977 and 1987 (see Figure 2.3). Not all of the local governments in the Urban West states abandoned the property tax as their major source of revenue. The local governments of two Urban West states, Oregon and Idaho, still rely on the property tax for over 90 percent of their total local tax collections (Idaho for 96.3 percent in 1987; Oregon for 90.3 percent in 1987). Oregon's reliance on the property tax needs to be reassessed, however, in light of its new constitutional property tax-reduction amendment known as Measure 5. The Oregon Legislative Revenue Office estimated that by 1995–1996, the amount of money collected through the property tax will have declined 55 percent under Measure 5 (Weber, 1990).

The immediate impact of the late 1970s and early 1980s property tax-limitation measures is also evident in the average per capita revenue generated from property taxes among the thirty-four Urban West medium-sized cities. As Table 2.3 indicates, the average per capita property tax revenue fell from $107.99 in 1977 to only $77.04 in 1982.

Turning now to our focus cities, the impact of these property tax-limitations measures can be seen in the case of Reno, Nevada, which experienced a loss of revenue and employees as a result of the implementation of its tax shift law. Nevada's 1981 tax shift law includes a limitation on the growth of revenue for local governments that ties that growth to the addition of new property on the tax rolls and inflation. It reduced property taxes by 20 percent and attempted to compensate for this loss by increasing sales tax allocations to cities. However, the compensation was not adequate. City revenue and the number of employees declined. In 1977, Reno had approximately 1,500 employees. In 1981, following the implementation of the new law, the number of city employees dropped to 995. Since 1981, the city has also been forced to transfer approximately $12 million of capital outlay funds in order to balance its operating budgets. Throughout the remainder of the 1980s, the city was never able to adopt a balanced budget, and it has become increasingly dependent on outside funding sources. Almost 45 percent of the city's general fund is composed of intergovernmental revenue, most of which is state aid (Reno Finance Department, 1989).

Another example of the fiscal impacts of a property tax-limitation law can be found in Boise, Idaho. The passage of property tax-limitation measures in Idaho had a serious effect on service delivery in the Boise area (see Figure 2.4). Even though Boise is one of the fastest-growing cities in the country, it did not have as many public safety employees in 1990 as it did in 1978, the year prior to the passage of Idaho's 1 percent initiative. From fiscal years 1979 to 1990, the city increased in population by 25 percent and the taxable value of its property increased by over 100 percent, but the number of municipal employees essentially remained the same (Boise City Finance Department, 1990).

Despite predictions of its early demise, the tax revolt is still alive in the West. Although the 1990 election did not produce many new broad mandates for more limits, generally there remain strong efforts in many Western states to legislate additional controls on governmental growth and spending. Tax-limitation measures of one form or another were on the ballot in nine states, including the Western states of California, Colorado, Montana, Nevada, Oregon, South Dakota, and Utah. Only in Oregon and in Nevada did any major propositions pass. The victory in Nevada for the tax protestors was rather limited because Nevada voters approved a measure to prohibit the establishment of a personal income tax. The impact of Measure 5 in Oregon, however, is substantial in the short run and could become even more pronounced over the next several years. Proponents of property tax limitation in Idaho failed to pass an initiative that would have limited property taxes to 1 percent in 1992. However, in the same year in Colorado, property tax-limitation sponsors were successful after several failed attempts in passing a constitutional amendment.

Consideration of all of these limitations are critical to the understanding of the types of responses and capacities Urban West cities possess to manage growth or decline. Their degree of reliance on the property tax and the type of limitation that is not responsive to growth will make it difficult for communities to grow without a negative impact on both the quality and level of their public services.

GROWTH IN THE DECADE OF CHANGE

The final major change affecting the Urban West in our decade of change is growth. Growth in population presents both a benefit and a cost to cities. On the one hand, new population means new taxpayers. On the other, growth places new demands on already stretched city services and amenities. Growth is an important factor in the decade of change because adding population in a climate of federal aid cutbacks and tax limitations may mean that cities are forced to do more with less. Many cities face new demands and new conflicts over the impact of growth at the very time that their resource base is declining. The management of growth and conflicts over it are discussed more fully in chapters 3 and 6. This section briefly discusses Urban West growth as the final component of the decade of change.

The general growth in population in the West and the South has been well documented. Generally referred to as the Sunbelt, these regions of the country have experienced a significant increase in population over the last decades. There are many reasons for this population increase, such as substantial federal military spending in the region, federal funding for interstate highways connecting the cities in the region, and lower overall labor costs (see Sawers and Tabb [1984], for an overview of this subject). As a region, the area encompassing the *Urban West* study has benefited from this general growth trend. U.S. Census figures of 1990 indicate that the ten fastest-growing cities in the country (in terms of percentage gain in population) were in the West. Of the sixty fastest-growing cities (in terms of percentage gain in population), fifty-one were in the West. As Table 2.5 indicates, thirty of the thirty-four Urban West cities experienced significant growth in the twenty-year span between 1970 and 1990. Glendale, Arizona, grew an incredible 309 percent, while Bakersfield (151 percent), Modesto (149 percent), and Tempe (123 percent) also grew dramatically. The average percentage increases across all thirty-four Urban West cities for the period between 1970 and 1990 was 59 percent (see Table 2.5).

Growth in the West is widespread, but it is not uniform throughout all of its cities. This fact is reflected in some of the Urban West focus cities. Spokane and Tacoma's percentage increase in population was a modest 4 percent, and Salt Lake City's population declined 9 percent. Pueblo experienced a 1 percent decrease in population, and is one of only five Urban West cities above 100,000 in population in 1980 that fell below 100,000 by 1990. It should be noted, however, that, like many urban areas in the West, the Spokane, Salt Lake City, and Pueblo metropolitan statistical areas (MSAs) experienced growth even though their central cities registered little or no growth. The Spokane metropolitan area grew 4.3 percent from 1980 to 1988, the Tacoma metropolitan statistical area grew 15.1 percent, the Salt Lake City-Ogden area grew 17 percent, while the Pueblo metropolitan area grew a modest 1.3 percent (Ross, Levine, and Stedman, 1991). Growth around the perimeters of cities is common. It is perhaps doubly frustrating because with that growth comes additional demand for such city services as road, police, and fire, while the new commuters contribute nothing to the property tax coffers of the central cities affected.

CONCLUSION

Although all cities across the country may not have experienced the full force of all the demographic, intergovernmental, and fiscal changes occurring during the decade of 1978–1988, most cities of the Urban West were significantly affected by all of these changes. The dramatic decline in federal aid and the fiscal impact of the property tax revolts presented Western cities with a series of challenges that were only compounded by the significant demographic changes the region experienced. These external developments give credence to the notion that cities are limited. Many of the important urban developments during this decade had one distinguishing feature—changes happened to cities, as opposed to being initiated by them. Cities were primarily left in a reactive mode. Some

Figure 2.4
Boise City Employees Compared with Assessed Valuation and Population Increases

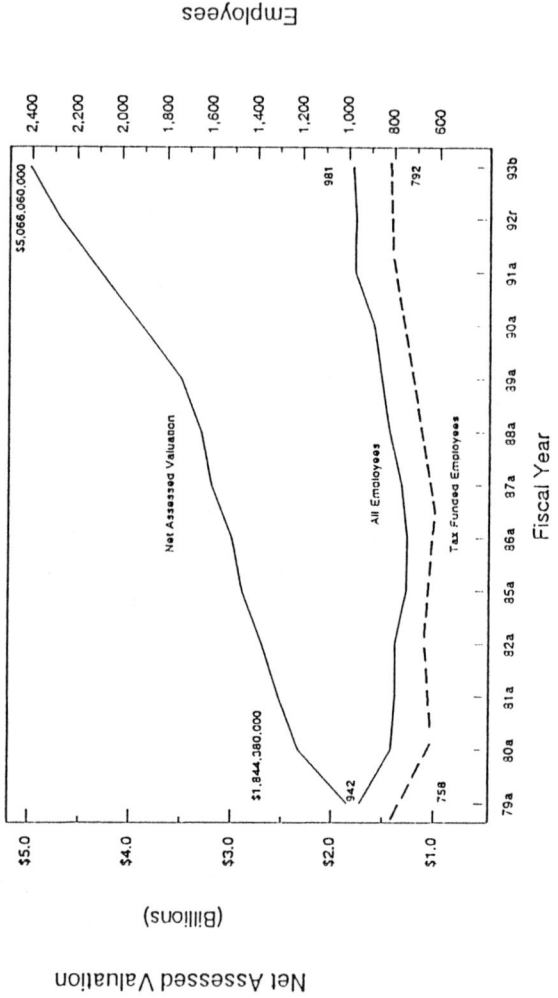

Boise City Employees
Compared to Net Assessed Valuation

32

Boise City Employees

Compared With Population from Fiscal Years 1979 through 1993

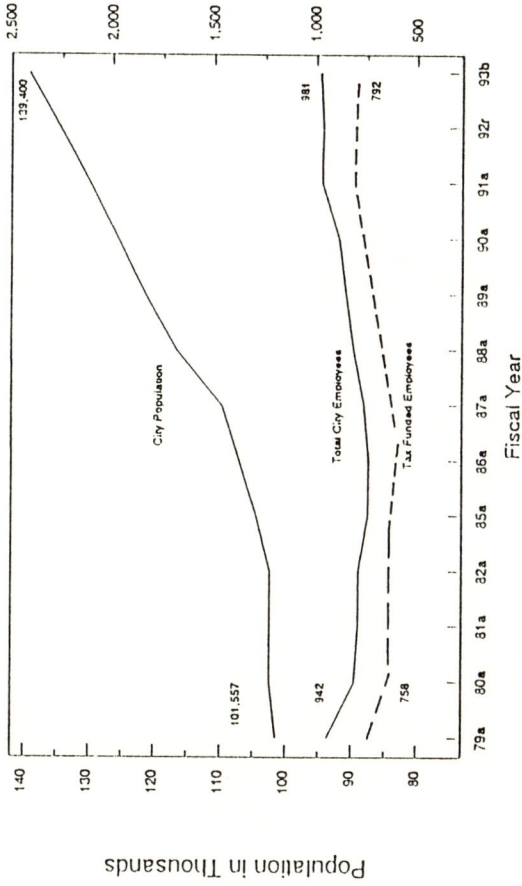

City Employees

Population in Thousands

Fiscal Year

City Population

139,400

101,557

Total City Employees

981

942

Tax Funded Employees

792

758

Source: Boise City Finance Department.

33

Table 2.5
Population and Growth Rate for Thirty-Four Western Cities, 1970–1990

| Cities | Population | | Percentage |
	1970	1990	Increase
1. Las Vegas	125,787	258,295	105%
2. Riverside	140,089	226,505	62
3. Stockton	109,963	210,943	92
4. Huntington	115,960	181,519	57
5. Glendale, CA	132,664	180,038	36
6. Spokane	170,516	177,196	4
7. Tacoma	154,407	176,664	14
8. Bakersfield	69,515	174,820	151
9. Fremont	100,869	173,339	72
10. Modesto	66,070	164,730	149
11. San Bernardino	109,203	164,164	50
12. Salt Lake City	175,885	159,936	-9
13. Glendale, AZ	36,228	148,134	309
14. Garden Grove	121,155	143,050	18
15. Oxnard	71,225	142,216	100
16. Tempe	63,550	141,865	123
17. Chula Vista	67,901	135,163	99
18. Reno	72,863	133,850	84
19. Ontario	64,118	133,179	107
20. Torrance	134,968	133,107	-1
21. Pasadena	112,951	131,591	17
22. Pomona	87,384	131,723	50
23. Lakewood, CO	92,787	126,481	36
24. Boise	84,429	125,738	49
25. Sunnyvale	95,976	117,229	22
26. Fullerton	85,987	114,144	33
27. Eugene	80,607	112,669	40
28. Hayward	93,058	111,498	20
29. Concord	85,164	111,348	31
30. Orange	77,365	110,658	43
31. Inglewood	89,985	109,602	22
32. Salem	72,194	107,786	50
33. Berkeley	114,091	102,724	-10
34. Pueblo	99,978	98,640	-1

Source: U.S. Bureau of the Census, selected years.

Figure 2.5
City of Spokane General Fund Revenue, 1990

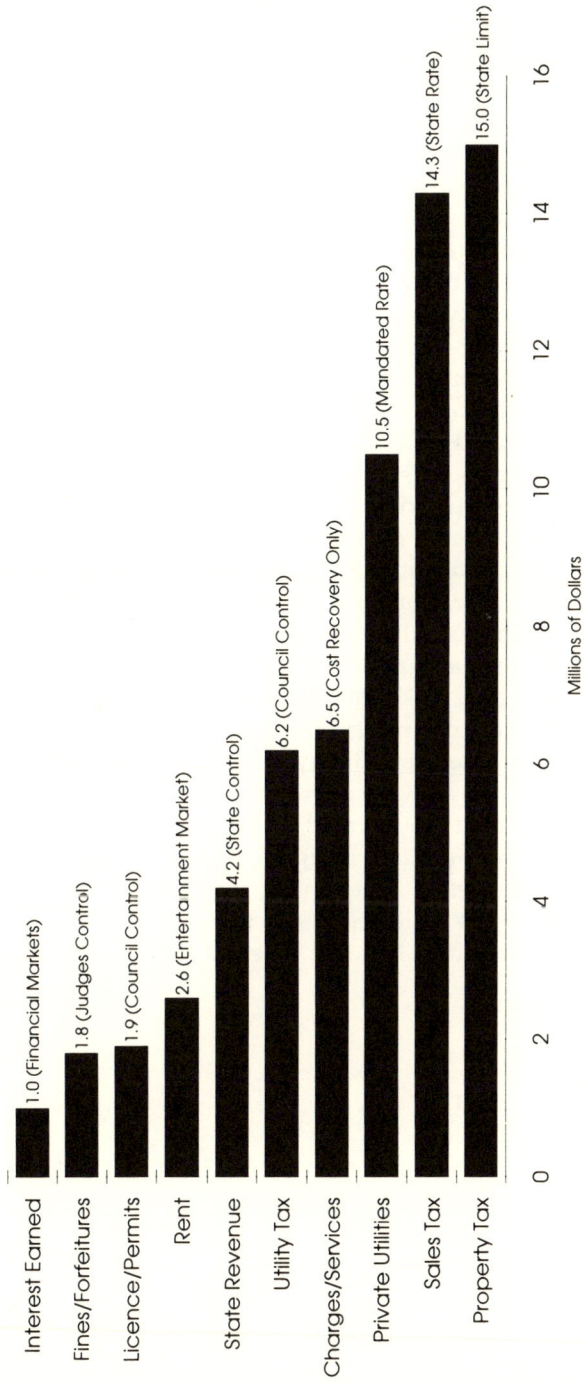

Interest Earned ▮ 1.0 (Financial Markets)

Fines/Forfeitures ▮ 1.8 (Judges Control)

Licence/Permits ▮ 1.9 (Council Control)

Rent ▮ 2.6 (Entertanment Market)

State Revenue ▮ 4.2 (State Control)

Utility Tax ▮ 6.2 (Council Control)

Charges/Services ▮ 6.5 (Cost Recovery Only)

Private Utilities ▮ 10.5 (Mandated Rate)

Sales Tax ▮ 14.3 (State Rate)

Property Tax ▮ 15.0 (State Limit)

0   2   4   6   8   10   12   14   16

Millions of Dollars

Source: City of Spokane.

35

were more successful in coping with the changes than others, but none had the luxury of avoiding the consequences of these changes.

We think that many of the economic and intergovernmental constraints that cities must operate within can be well illustrated by examining the budget of one of our focus cities, Spokane, Washington. Revenue sources for Spokane's general fund in 1990 are shown in Figure 2.5. The figure also indicates who has control over each of these revenue streams. There were ten major sources of revenue for Spokane city in 1990, yet only two of those sources were under the direct control of the city council. These two sources account for only 13 percent of the revenue used by the city. The effects of the property tax revolt are evident in the state-wide lid on property tax revenue. Spokane was collecting the top amount allowed under state law; consequently, that source of revenue cannot be increased by the city. The growing importance of state aid to local government is illustrated by the fact that 29 percent of the total city general-fund revenue comes from state-shared money. Additionally, the diminished federal role in city finance is illustrated by the fact that there is no federal component to Spokane's general-fund revenue.

Each of the major changes that occurred in the 1978–1988 period—the decline of federal aid, the property tax revolts, increasing mandates on cities, and uneven and rapid regional growth—would be significant in its impact on cities. Taken together, they represent a critical change in the demands and constraints placed on local governments. It is this set of changes that determines the problems currently faced by cities.

These problems, as well as growth, funding infrastructure, and economic development, are covered in the next chapters. Each of these policy areas will be examined in light of cities' limitations and challenges that we have discussed. When these new challenges are faced within the existing framework of limited powers given to cities in our system of federalism, it becomes clear that cities face a difficult task.

3

Coping with Growth

This chapter examines the policies and programs implemented by public officials in the Urban West to manage growth in their jurisdictions. Perspectives vary greatly among public officials and their constituents as to the relative costs and benefits of growth. As recently noted by a perceptive South Carolina city administrator, "growth is a curse or a golden opportunity, depending on the point of view of the observer. The visionary elected leader or public administrator sees growth as a coveted goal to be attained as quickly as possible. These officials stress the glamorous aspects—new jobs, expansion of the tax base, better housing and transportation, greater service for more people" (Broom, 1988:12).

The "curse" perspective holds that sustained growth, in particular, rapid growth, and the maintenance of a high quality of life are mutually exclusive goals. Substantial growth can give rise to air and water pollution, traffic congestion, crowded park and recreational facilities, rising housing prices, displacement of established neighborhoods and other negative effects. An article in a *Seattle Times* supplement that discussed public issues occasioned by explosive growth in the Puget Sound area captured the fears of many mid-size communities trying to cope with growth effectively. The article read in part: "Do you know the way to San Jose? It's simple: annex more, plan less density and develop, de-

velop, develop" (Peirce and Johnson, 1989:6). There are significant financial consequences to growth as well. The "curse" perspective holds that
existing public service levels often suffer a decline when services are
extended to new properties and populations without the necessary revenue to fund such extensions. In short, according to this perspective,
growth that does not "pay its own way" should be opposed.

The "golden opportunity" perspective is based on the notion that
growth is a positive benefit, if not a panacea, that more than pays for
itself, and that everyone benefits from growth. According to a Boise economic development advocate, "economic growth means opportunity—
opportunity for personal growth and economic security for the present
and following generations. It means the money to finance the arts, to
enjoy recreation, and to improve education for both children and adults.
A community without economic growth is one short on opportunity"
(Barber, 1992:1F).

Given the prevalence of aggressive municipal economic development
campaigns throughout the country (discussed more fully in chapter 6),
and certainly reflected in most of our Urban West focus cities, it appears
that many officials would agree with former Boise Mayor Dirk Kempthorne (1990), who believed that growth is an essential component of a
community's quality of life. In one of his speeches, he expressed the
view, shared by many Western municipal leaders, that "economic vitality and quality of life are not mutually exclusive. Economic vitality is
part of quality of life."

As this chapter will discuss, however, the timing, location, and intensity of growth are only partially under the control of city hall. Paul Peterson (1981) noted that cities are not nation-states and cannot control
the movement of capital and people across their boundaries. Cities can
and do offer enticements to attract growth, but the potential investors
have to choose *your* city. The frustrations of coaxing, bargaining with,
and, finally, relenting to the locational decisions of businesses considering Boise are detailed in this chapter's first case study.

Despite the fact that Boise's former mayor embraced both growth and
quality of life as complementary, his view of the compatibility between
economic vitality (growth) and quality of life was clearly not shared by
every Boisean, especially those neighborhood activists who have worked
hard to stop proposed foothill developments within Boise. (See later in
this chapter the case study: Boise, Idaho—The Growth/Quality of Life
Pendulum.)

There are many actions that can be taken to address the "curses" of
growth described above. There is little agreement, however, on what
kinds of policies work best. Some fear that efforts to limit or direct
growth will chase away jobs. Others worry that growth management will
hurt the value of their property. On the other hand, proponents of

growth management warn that, without action, the quality of life that brought people to the community will be lost. These conflicting perspectives on growth and growth management are described in this chapter in the Modesto case study, Citizens Respond to Rapid Growth, which describes the adoption of a growth-limiting measure in that city.

The Modesto case highlights the fact that choices about how to handle growth come not only from city council chambers, but also from the citizens directly. In our democratic system, and especially in the West, citizens can pass growth-management measures by initiative. Measure A, described in the case, was passed by the initiative process. Not all citizen activity, of course, leads to an initiative. The efforts of neighborhood groups to affect growth decisions can be found in several of the Urban West focus cities.

Managing growth is also clearly a function of our complex intergovernmental system. City officials make growth-management decisions in a context of state laws setting out municipal powers and dictating certain actions. Two important sources of state control over growth management—annexation laws and state growth-management legislation—are also explained in this chapter.

Growth-management legislation and land-use policy in general continue to be two of the most volatile issues faced by state and local decision makers throughout the Urban West. In this chapter we look at some of the techniques used by cities and states to manage growth effectively, and we examine some of the conflicts that have arisen over growth and growth management in our Urban West cities.

CASE STUDY: BOISE, IDAHO—THE GROWTH/QUALITY OF LIFE PENDULUM

Balancing a high quality of life with steady economic growth has been the challenge in Boise, Idaho's capital city. This southwestern Idaho city is the seat of state and county government, the home of Boise State University, and the headquarters of some of the nation's largest corporations—Albertson's, Boise Cascade, Micron Technology, Morrison-Knudsen, J. R. Simplot, TJ International, and Ore-Ida Foods. Several of Hewlett-Packard's divisions have their headquarters in Boise.

Over the past twenty years, the pendulum has swung back and forth between public support for slow- and rapid-growth policies. The direction of the pendulum's swing has largely been determined by the nation and the community's economic health, and the extent of the effects growth has had on public services and important quality-of-life components.

During the late 1970s, uncontrolled growth and urban sprawl were atop the list of the community's concerns (Barber, 1992; Warbis, 1990). Proposals for the implementation of growth-management measures and growth-impact fees were seriously debated. The city adopted a major planning document, the Boise Metropolitan Plan, which directed growth toward the Southeast and away from the unfolding sprawl in the West. The mayor reaffirmed his goal of "retaining downtown Boise as the regional shopping center [and stopping] the suburban sprawl [that] has ruined so many other cities in this country" (Eardley, 1975:4). Clearly, city officials wanted to avert the "mistakes" of other cities whose downtowns were deserted as a consequence of the flight to the suburbs.

Growth took place in Southeastern Boise as planned, but the urban sprawl feared to the West of the city has continued—much of it outside city limits. Boise suffered greatly from the effects of a national recession in the early 1980s and failed during that period in its effort to convince reluctant major retailers to commit themselves to the building of a downtown regional shopping mall. These retailers generally succeeded in avoiding pressures by local officials in other states and located their new stores in the suburbs away from the downtown areas. They apparently concluded that they could do the same thing in Boise despite city commitment to the downtown area. Those who did agree to start up businesses in a downtown location were in a strong negotiating position to make significant demands on city officials. For instance, J. C. Penney Corp. insisted on the enclosed mall, even though a majority of Boiseans found the idea unfavorable (Hanson and Scheffer, 1975). Echoes of Peterson's limited city can be read into Mayor Eardley's (1975) lament during his negotiations with the retailers. He observed that "the future of this city and its shopping area [will be] dependent almost entirely on an outside firm" (p. 5). Despite a commitment to a twenty-year goal of building the major retail center in downtown Boise, public officials could not succeed because the major decisions affecting the downtown were being made in corporate board rooms across America rather than in the city council meetings and voting booths of Boise, Idaho.

During the bad economic times of the early 1980s, Boise voters were markedly more willing to elect development-oriented local officials than they were in the more prosperous years of the decade. The new Mayor Dirk Kempthorne and new council members were told "to do something even if it's wrong" (Kempthorne, 1990). Economic vitality became the dominant policy goal during the balance of the 1980s. Concerns about sprawl and keeping a vibrant downtown gave way to a need to stimulate the local economy. A common refrain for a number of local politicians was that planning should not stand in the way of growth (R. Fuhrman, 1990). The city council amended the Boise Metro Plan and allowed the building of a mall in the suburbs but still within the city limits. This decision seemed to unclog the twenty-year planning logjam in economic activity in Boise. Sales at the mall and construction throughout the area have exceeded all expectations. New high-tech firms were attracted to

Boise and several locally based businesses have expanded their operations significantly. Boise in the early 1990s is among the top population gainers in the country. The *1990 Small Business Survey Report* predicted that Boise would be among the fifteen top cities in the country with respect to population growth in the next five years (R. Fuhrman, 1990). In addition, several national magazines have highlighted Boise as one of the most desirable places to live in the United States (Hamburg, 1992).

High ratings on both livability and economic scales indicate that, at least in the minds of some national reporters, the growth and quality-of-life equation is somewhat in balance in Boise. It is true, now that the general economic situation of the metropolitan area is improving, that other quality-of-life considerations are getting greater attention. An old issue is again on the front burner: How can this growth be made to pay its fair share? Managed growth is again a dominant goal. Transportation impact fees were implemented in 1992, and other similar fees may follow. Growth is again seen in all its complexity—the good along with the bad. Amenities added by growth such as an expanded tax base and greater recreational and cultural activities are evident, but so are crowded schools, dirtier air, longer waits for service, more crime, and congested streets. A recent survey indicates that a majority of Boiseans want the growth rate to be cut in half (Lyman, 1991). Planning is again being emphasized. Hundreds of Boiseans were involved in a major grassroots planning effort whose results were recently published in *Boise Visions Final Report*. The intent of this process was to develop a long-range plan that would secure a balanced future for Boise with all of its quality-of-life components nicely in place.

Can Boise have it all? Former Mayor Kempthorne (1990) thought so. He called himself a "pro-business environmentalist" mayor. Only the future will tell whether this label was a stroke of genius or an oxymoron. Even though it was 1979 when Boise Cascade President John Fery said it, there is still a belief that "[t]ime is still on our side—but just barely. . . . If we can manage the growth that is upon us, make the right decisions about it—everybody will win" (p. 22).

LIMITED CITIES

In formulating and implementing growth-management policies and programs, cities are limited in their ability to determine their own destiny. *City Limits*, by Paul Peterson (1981), is not only the title of an important work on urban policy making, but also an apt description of the limited powers available to municipal decision makers in this country. Municipal home rule and local autonomy are indeed important for the internal operation of cities. However, their significance pales in comparison to the weight of federal mandates, state limits, and the vagaries of economic forces. As chapter 2 described, the environment for many cities has become quite hostile, with citizens demanding lower taxes and more services, all against a backdrop of declining federal support for urban programs and revenue transfers.

What sorts of tools are available to Western cities to manage growth, given the economic and intergovernmental limits within which they must work? An analysis of these techniques demonstrates that cities as political actors have only a handful of tools to control and direct growth. Other intergovernmental actors, including national and state governments, counties, and neighborhood groups, also enact policies that limit a city's choices (Glickfeld and Levine, 1992). In this chapter we examine the sorts of growth-management techniques that are currently in use nationally and among the Urban West cities. This analysis addresses growth-management tools that are imposed by the state, imposed by the citizens through initiatives and neighborhood groups, or adopted by the city government itself.

STATE-IMPOSED LIMITS ON CITIES

Since Judge Dillon's assertion of state supremacy in state-local relations in 1868, Dillon's Rule has been accepted as precedent by the courts to narrowly construe the exercise of municipal powers. Cities have been considered creatures of their states, with only those powers given to them by their state legislature or state constitution (*City of Clinton v. Cedar Rapids and Missouri River Railroad Co.*, 1868). No examination of growth management within urban areas can be complete without addressing the limitations imposed by the state legislatures and courts on local units of government. Although there are many ways in which state actions can limit cities' options in managing growth, such as the creation of metropolitan service districts or consolidation of city and county governments, there are two direct actions that will be discussed here in detail: state laws outlining city annexation powers and legislation mandating growth-management processes and policies.[1]

State Annexation Laws and Their Impact on Cities

One method of coping with growth available to many cities is to annex adjacent land in order to enlarge the corporate boundaries of the municipality. There are many reasons for cities to attempt annexation, some of the most important being the provision of orderly growth and development of the city, the extension of services to adjacent properties, the preemption of the creation of another city or another governmental entity, the denial of the properties to another city, the expansion of the city's tax base, and the promotion of economic development.

Whatever the municipal motivation might be, annexation is a particularly important planning tool for cities. It is through the annexation process that cities can sometimes control their preferred plans for expansion and greatly influence the quality of growth permitted within an area. Policies that tie annexation to service delivery are particularly effective in this regard. If the city will not extend services to a developing unincorporated area without an agreement to be annexed, or if state law allows it to unilaterally annex, then city officials have major control over the shape and quality of development within an area. General-purpose governments like cities have the capability to deliver a range of services to developing urban fringe areas. Unlike special-purpose districts and most counties, cities have the authority to provide the menu of urban services that are necessary for densely populated areas. Service delivered by one government, rather than by many, tends to avoid problems of unclear accountability and duplicated services that so often plague metropolitan areas where cities cannot easily grow.

The tax-base expansion and mitigation of service costs are also important reasons for why cities decide to annex. Highly valued properties with relatively low service demands result in a revenue surplus to the city. This is particularly the case with annexations that include major commercial and industrial sites with little residential property. Another aspect of the service cost–revenue generation equation is the concern that residents of adjacent properties already enjoy the use of many city services. Often they work in the city, or at least spend a great deal of time within the city, without making significant contributions to the funding of city services. They also benefit from mutual aid agreements many cities have with rural fire districts and other service deliverers operating within an urbanized area. The bottom line is that city property taxpayers pick up the tab for services delivered to a much larger population than lives within the city. In Salt Lake City, for example, the approximately 160,000 residents are largely responsible for funding the services to the approximately 140,000 additional people who "live" in the city during the day. With the limited revenue options available to municipal officials in Salt Lake City, daytime residents have little "opportunity" to pay for the services and facilities they use.

Economic development is another reason for annexation. The City of Pueblo annexed an industrial park at its airport so that city services could be extended to attract new businesses. The provision of these services is critical to the success of Pueblo's aggressive economic development strategy (see the Pueblo case study in chapter 6). A feature of Idaho's property tax-limitation law, which was in effect from 1979 to 1986, did not allow cities to add, for budgeting purposes, all of the value of annexed properties to its tax base. Once state legislators clearly understood the anti-growth aspects of this limitation, they changed it. Even one of the most vocal property tax crusaders in the state, a state senator from Boise in 1986, voted for this particular change when she understood the adverse economic impacts of such a restriction.

The surplus or revenue gain created by an annexation is often subject to question. City officials sometimes err by focusing more on anticipated revenues rather than fully analyzing the myriad services costs that are not always evident. An area with a substantial market value might provide just enough population or distance from a fire station, for example, to require that the city build a new station if it is to maintain its current fire rating. The additional revenue generated by the newly annexed properties often provides, however, an important new source of revenue to the operating budget. However, an offsetting requirement to build a new million-dollar fire station might quickly make such an annexation unattractive.

The City of Boise has faced such dilemmas and has been able to address some of these problems through the implementation of mutual aid agreements with rural fire-protection districts operating in the area prior to the annexation. With some annexations, the city entered into a mutual aid agreement that requires back-up response in emergency situations and allows the rural fire district to, for the time being, keep one of its own fire stations in operation instead of closing it due to the loss of territory and tax base resulting from the annexation (Gerber, 1987).

State laws limit the ability of the city to annex by establishing the procedures by which cities may take in new territory. Even in home rule cities like Pueblo, state law preempts the exercise of local discretionary authority (Munch, personal communication, June 26, 1990). The complexity of these procedures and the difficulties they impose on cities undertaking such actions vary widely throughout the country. In only a few states is annexation relatively easy, allowing the city council to annex adjacent territories by ordinance (Bollens and Schmandt, 1975).

In a majority of the states, cities are required to do one or more of the following: gain approval from the voters in the area to be annexed either through a petition or a referendum; seek approval from another governmental entity; submit the proposed annexation to judicial determination; or hold a public hearing.[2] According to conventional wisdom, the more stringent the annexation procedures, the less likely a city will be successful in annexation (Fleischmann, 1986). Conventional wisdom is founded in the historical reality that in the early years of this century, legislatures dominated by rural interests, fearing the growth of cities, began imposing significant constraints on the ability of cities to extend their boundaries. Prior to 1900, municipal annexation generally kept pace with the growth in population. But the rise of immigration, big city corruption, and rapid city growth led many rural legislators, fearful of the potential of city domination, to make annexation much more difficult.

Correspondingly, many states made incorporation of small cities easier, thus limiting the growth of many of the larger cities, particularly those in the Northeast (Colman, 1975).

According to Bollens and Schmandt (1975:241), "annexation procedures were made extremely complex by giving the property owners or voters in the unincorporated territory the exclusive right to begin the annexation or by requiring a popular majority in the affected area to approve the absorption." An editorial comment in a 1977 edition of *Tennessee Town & City* magazine effectively summarizes the conventional wisdom concerning these anti-city state legislative acts: "Core cities everywhere else are dying on the vine because they cannot grow. Their city limits are fixed. Their suburbs are separate jurisdictions and, as such, they deny the central city that base in people and property, that vital leadership, those revenue sources, without which municipal survival is impossible" (Lovelace, 1977:10).

In spite of these restrictive state laws, some annexation has still occurred. At least two studies suggest that the relationship between restrictive annexation laws and the slowing down of annexation activity is tenuous at best (Dye, 1964; MacManus and Thomas, 1979). One study, however, found that cities with more liberal annexation laws are somewhat more prone to attempt annexation than those without such laws (Wheeler, 1965). Fleischmann (1986:139) found "that while annexation procedures may affect cities' expansion strategies, they are not insurmountable obstacles." Some of this success can be attributed to the commitment of the city officials to make the proposed annexation attractive to the residents of an urban fringe area and to make them aware of the additional municipal services that would be available to them as city residents. A good example of city officials promoting the benefits of city residency occurred during a long period at the turn of the century when there was relatively little annexation in the country. In contrast to the rest of the nation, there was considerable activity in the Los Angeles area because the city was able to use "control of the area's major water supply as an enticement . . . to persuade a number of municipalities to consolidate with it" (Bollens and Schmandt, 1975:239–40).

Other variables appear to be more closely correlated with levels of annexation than the relative stringency of annexation statutes. State property tax-limitation statutes that do not allow the city to generate additional revenue from the annexed properties severely dampen city interest in expansion, even when residents of the adjoining areas or real estate developers are urgently requesting such annexation. A good example of this situation is the experience of the City of Boise. During periods of significant growth on its urban fringe area during much of the 1980s, the city, even though it had unilateral annexation powers, did not pursue an aggressive annexation policy. It did not do so because the

property tax-limitation law in effect at that time did not allow the city
to collect all of the additional revenue such an expansion ordinarily
would generate. As soon as that law was changed by the addition of a
growth amendment in 1986, Boise city officials began implementing an
aggressive annexation strategy that lasted through the balance of the
1980s (Gerber, 1987).

The unilateral annexation authority enjoyed by city officials in Idaho,
Tennessee, and Texas is the envy of the nation's municipal officials. The
policy statements of many state municipal leagues indicate that one of
their high priorities is the relaxation or repeal of anti-annexation laws
that are perceived to make annexation very difficult, if not impossible.
The policy statement of the Kansas Municipal League reflects most state
municipal league positions and effectively summarizes the high degree
of municipal frustration over restrictive annexation laws in most states:

> The owners or residents of land adjoining the city should not be
> granted a statutory right to vote on or consent to annexation. It is
> essential that the long-term public interest of the whole community
> be given priority in municipal growth, in the same manner that
> other, over-all community needs in an urban society occasionally
> require the sacrifice of some private goals and interests in order to
> achieve the greatest social utility of the area and benefits to the
> many. It is untenable that the owners of land within the fringe area,
> whose location has benefits primarily in relation to the existence of
> the city, should be given veto power over the geographic, eco-
> nomic, and governmental destiny of the city. (Mosher, 1982:47)

No one single variable or circumstance can fully account for annexation activity. State statutes may not have the constraining effects that the
conventional wisdom would suggest. It should not go unnoticed, however, that municipal policy makers believe these statutes represent an
important impediment and that they have fought hard across the country
to relax these restrictions where they are in effect.

The two regions of the country that have undertaken the most annexations in recent years are the West and the South (Miller and Forstall,
1984). Clearly, the states of the Sunbelt have done fairly well in expanding their boundaries to accommodate the growth they have experienced
over the past two decades. In fact, "virtually all the largest annexations
in the 1970s and 1980s took place in the Sunbelt" (Ross et al., 1991:301).
Two primary reasons are suggested for the more aggressive annexation
activity having occurred in the metropolitan and urbanized areas of the
West and the South. First, state laws in these areas generally allow ex-
traterritorial powers to 'keep nearby land unincorporated and available
for annexation," and second, there is usually a smaller socioeconomic

difference between Sunbelt inner cities and their suburbs, thereby less-ening suburban resistance to annexation (Ross et al., p. 303).

State Growth-Management Laws

Although states have historically had little, if any, direct role in local land-use planning, in some states urban growth has been so disruptive that the state has assumed a greater role in monitoring and directing the actions of local governments to control or manage growth (Chinitz, 1990). As noted in the prior section, cities are limited in their ability to annex land, and growth often occurs in the unincorporated county sur-rounding the city. This places new demands on county governments, some of which are ill-prepared to deliver urban-level services. Rapid growth has often resulted in traffic congestion, lack of school space, and regional problems in dealing with air quality, water quality, sewage treatment, and solid waste (garbage) disposal. As urban areas expand, lands traditionally used for farming, forested lands and fragile coastal areas are developed for housing and service uses. These problems are difficult to manage given the fragmented nature of local government, and some states have stepped in to provide state-wide framework for managing growth and some types of land-use decisions. Legislation of this type is usually referred to as a growth-management law.

As of April 1991, nine states had adopted comprehensive state growth-management laws: Hawaii, Florida, Vermont, New Jersey, Maine, Rhode Island, Georgia, Oregon, and Washington (Neumann, 1991). To some, state growth-management laws represent a loss of local autonomy to the extent that they impose a set of decision-making rules on local govern-ments, or, in some cases, dictate the content of local decisions about growth and land uses. State growth-management legislation can indeed represent a serious limitation on the powers of cities to make land-use decisions as they wish. However, these laws may sometimes empower cities with new authority to shape their physical size, level of service provision, and quality of life. While each of these state laws is rather distinctive, they do share certain components and approaches. Neumann (1991) points out that all nine states with growth-management laws share the following planning goals: affordable housing provision, economic development, agricultural preservation, water quality protection, multi-modal transportation system, historic preservation, natural resource con-servation, and open-space preservation. As described above, these are often the sorts of issues that "fall through the cracks" in a rapidly grow-ing area. To achieve these goals, the states utilize a variety of require-ments, processes, and inducements for cities. Some of these components are discussed in the next section.

Requirements to Plan. Most state-level growth-management laws require local governments to develop and adopt comprehensive plans. Plans developed at the local level may be required to be consistent with state goals for planning or with the plans of other local entities. At least two major challenges for local governments can result from these planning requirements. The first is that many municipalities lack the staff, expertise, and resources to comply successfully with new state requirements to plan. Decker's (1987:47) study of non-metropolitan counties in Florida, for example, concluded that many lacked "managerial and organizational capacities for effective growth management as mandated by the state of Florida." The Washington State Growth Management Strategies Commission (1990) estimated that it will require $50 million to $60 million in the period 1991–1995 to develop initial local plans required under that state's growth-management legislation. Given the persistent lack of growth in state and local revenue in recent years, this additional need will be difficult to meet.

A second challenge involves the increased intergovernmental cooperation necessitated by most growth-management legislation. Neumann (1991) indicates that the process for achieving intergovernmental cooperation is usually specified in the state growth-management legislation, or handled more informally by a state agency. Some plans require regional approaches to problems, while other components of growth management, such as the designation of urban growth boundaries (discussed below), require city–county negotiation and substantive agreement on planning issues. Many local officials may lack familiarity, skills, or disposition to develop the intergovernmental relationships necessary for effective growth management. The challenging nature of the planning, negotiation, and changes required under growth-management legislation can engender much conflict as cities, counties, and special districts wrestle with regional problems.

Conflict, however, need not be a necessary byproduct of growth management. Washington's growth-management law, for example, and the recommendations of the State's Growth Management Commission, "make mediated dispute resolution an expected part of growth management in Washington State" (R. Faas, personal communication, March 1, 1991). A recent report identifies strategies to avoid conflict among local governments and the state, including examples from Georgia, Florida and Washington (Kartez, 1991). Wright (1988) found in his classic work on intergovernmental relations that governmental actors are increasingly looking toward negotiation and other forms of alternative dispute resolution (as opposed to litigation or inaction) to solve intergovernmental problems. Innovative local government-training programs, such as that conceived by the Program for Local Government Education (PGLE) in Washington state, now focus on building the skills of local government officials to carry out cooperative efforts aimed at solving multijurisdictional problems (Kartez, 1991). These skills become critical in light of the fact that several state growth-management laws require the development of a regional plan that addresses regional service needs such as transportation, housing, intrusive land-use siting, and capital facilities.

As noted above, state growth-management laws usually include the imposition of explicit state goals to be addressed in locally and regionally developed plans. For example, the Oregon State Land Conservation and Development Commission (LCDC) (1985) administers the implementation of eighteen land-use and planning goals that apply to all local governments in the state. They include items such as:

Goal #2. *Planning*: To establish land use planning process and policy framework as a basis for all decisions and actions related to the use of land and to assure an adequate factual base for such decisions and practices.

Goal #5. *Open Spaces, Scenic and Historic Areas, and Natural Resources*: To conserve open space and protect natural and scenic resources. (p. 1)

Each of the goals is followed by definitions and guidelines for planning and implementation to be used by the local governments. Naturally, the establishment of these goals and guidelines can be a very contentious process, as affected interest groups such as home builders or foresters, cities fearing loss of autonomy, and citizens fearing loss of control over the use of their property all seek to influence the details of growth management implementation.

Urban Growth Boundaries. Another component of state growth-management plans is the identification of an "urban growth boundary." Although many cities have adopted some sort of sphere of influence or urban growth boundary, in some states the negotiation and creation of these boundaries is mandated within a growth-management law. Typically, the urban growth boundary is intended to establish what the geographical and population size of the city will be at some future time—for example, in a fifty- or one-hundred-year time frame. Other approaches to the identification of an urban growth boundary assume a size at build-out, that is some optimal size in the foreseeable future (Kelly, 1988).

Urban growth boundaries can be used to limit or control sprawl, since new developments can be directed to the areas designated for urban levels of development. Most urban growth boundaries require the city to negotiate this future boundary with the county government, and establish standards of service within this area that will aid in its eventual annexation. In Oregon (and Idaho, although there is no comprehensive growth-management legislation), for example, the urban growth boundaries also establish the convention of the city providing urban services within that area targeted for eventual inclusion within the city's corporate limits. Critics of this type of land-use planning say that state-mandated growth management is too top-heavy, as evidenced by the fact that in Oregon, for example, a redrawing of the urban growth boundary for Salem would require the approval of the state-level Land Conservation and Development Commission (K. Battaille, personal communication, March 6, 1991).

Protection of Land Uses. Another common component of growth-management laws is the protection of certain types of land and land uses. Protected lands usually include open spaces, coastal areas, forested areas, estuarine areas, agricultural lands, and greenways or greenbelts. All of the previously mentioned growth-management laws include protection of various of these environmentally sensitive categories. Local governments are usually asked to inventory these protected lands in their jurisdiction and demonstrate that their land-use plans protect them from the effects of further development. Naturally, the definition of these protected classifications of land can be highly contentious, and sometimes encounter local opposition, particularly if a local economy is threatened. Counties and local economies dependent on revenue from timber sales, for example, may resist state requirements that forested lands be protected. Similarly, many home builders believe that open-space requirements too greatly limit opportunities to build new subdivisions.

State growth-management laws also mandate certain types of land uses in local and regional plans, such as the provision of low-income housing and adequate transportation infrastructure. Rapid growth in an area often results in the replacement of low-income housing with more profitable developments. The provision of adequate amounts of housing for middle- and lower-income workers becomes difficult. Many workers begin commuting from long distances, compounding traffic congestion problems and air pollution. Growth-management laws often require local governments to construct an inventory of available residential land and plan for provision of their proportionate share of low-income housing.

Transportation is often a regional issue, since many communities rely on shared networks of state and federal highways for their transportation needs. Rapid growth requires not just the planned expansion of existing highways, but also planning for alternative methods of transportation such as light rail or mass transit. Growth-management plans not only demand regional cooperation in planning for transportation needs, but also may require that new development be delayed until adequate services, including transportation, are in place. This issue of the pace of development is discussed further in chapter 5.

Carrots and Sticks from State-Mandated Growth Management. Along with state mandates that cities and counties participate in growth-management processes often come new authorities for revenue collection. These are the "carrots" that states hold out to entice cities to comply with these state growth-management laws. Chief among these new authorities is the developer impact fee. Impact fees can generally be defined as "charges collected by a locality during its review of land projects to support infrastructure needed to serve the proposed development" (Cervero, 1988: 535). These fees can be assessed to address infrastructure needs of many sorts, including roads, sewer and water facilities, storm drainage, schools, and parks. Several of the state growth-management laws discussed in this book give cities the authority to assess impact fees.

In Florida, for example, such fees are designed to ensure concurrency, that is, to require infrastructure to keep pace with new development. New development is not allowed until concurrency is ensured across a wide range of services such as roads, schools, sewer and water, and so on (Florida State Department of Community Affairs, 1989). This policy of concurrency is discussed in more detail in chapter 5. Other new taxes or revenue sources may be created or allowed under state growth-management legislation as an inducement for cities to comply with the requirements. An example here is the local real estate excise tax for capital improvements provided under the Washington State Growth Management Act (Association of Washington Cities [AWC], 1990). Finally, there may be state funding to assist in the development and administration of local and regional plans.

The "sticks" available to states to ensure compliance with growth-management legislation include, first, the withholding of the above new revenue sources if implementation requirements are not met. In some states, such as Florida and Oregon, sanctions are available to the state to ensure compliance from local units of government. In others, the state provides grants to local governments for planning as incentives to plan, which are withdrawn if the local governments fail to comply with the growth-management legislation. Continued compliance with the legislation is monitored through state-level reviews, which may be required before certain changes in land-use plans are allowed at the local level.

LOCAL GROWTH-MANAGEMENT OPTIONS

There are several ways in which local governments can act to limit or manage growth. An important mechanism for directing or limiting growth comes through the use of the zoning powers of the city. Johnson (1989:39) defines zoning "in its simplest sense, [as] the division of land into distinct use categories, permitting specified ones and excluding others." Recent court cases have held that communities that are in the path of growth must take their fair share of low-income housing and other services that must be provided on a regional basis (see New Jersey's three Mount Laurel cases: *Southern Burlington County NAACP v. Township of Mt. Laurel*, 1975; *Burlington County NAACP v. Township of Mount Laurel*, 1983; and *Hills Development Co. v. Township of Bernard*, 1986). The use of zoning, however, remains a powerful tool used to control the uses and densities cities will permit within their boundaries. Although most city planners who are trying to avoid sprawl would advocate the use of high-density uses within the city, some city officials and neighborhood groups organize around the principle of the low-density zoning to limit growth. This section of the chapter will look at the use of low-density zoning among the Urban West cities to limit growth.

A second way in which local governments may act to control growth is through the adoption of time- or area-specific moratoria on the issuance of building permits. Limits such as these are sometimes activated within the confines of state growth-management laws if concurrency of infrastructure with development is not met. Other communities, such as Petaluma, California, have adopted building moratoria in an attempt to put the brakes on rapid development (Kelly, 1988).

A third local growth-management technique is to put into place requirements that infrastructure keep pace with development. This is obviously related to the use of building permit moratoria as discussed above, but may include other pace-keeping requirements as well. In several states, cities are empowered to assess impact fees, which help ensure that the rate of development does not outpace the city's infrastructure. Although specific state authorization for the power to assess impact fees is recommended to survive court challenges, it is not required (Cervero, 1988).

A fourth way in which cities may manage growth is through the adoption of a specific annexation policy. While annexation powers are defined by the state as discussed above, cities may, within that general framework, adopt policies regarding when and how often they will annex properties. Many cities require citizens receiving city services, for example, to agree to later annex to the city without resistance (Leutwiler, 1987). This can help cities maintain practical areas of city service provision.

Local Citizen-Based Growth Management

The city government may not be the only local actor seeking to limit or control growth. In cities in which a local initiative process is available, neighborhood groups may institute new growth-management policies through the petition and special election process. Neighborhood groups are not limited, however, to the initiative process to get their policy preferences across to decision makers. Many activities are based on testifying at planning and zoning hearings and attempting to marshal support for their positions through the media. To gauge the amount of neighborhood or citizen activity directed toward limiting growth, we asked planning departments in the ten Urban West focus cities to indicate whether their citizens had used the initiative process to limit growth, and whether there were active neighborhood groups concerned with limiting growth in their city.

GROWTH MANAGEMENT IN THE TEN URBAN WEST FOCUS CITIES

Table 3.1 displays the various growth-management strategies in use in the ten Urban West focus cities. This display includes growth-management limits imposed by states as well as those adopted by cities themselves or imposed on them by citizen action. This table illustrates the principle that growth management, like many fiscal matters, is an arena within which cities confront many constraints. Growth-management policies may be voluntarily adopted by cities, but they can also be imposed on them either by the state or their own citizens.

Use of State-Imposed Growth Management

In two of the eight Urban West states, comprehensive state-level growth-management laws have been enacted into law (Oregon and Washington). As already noted, this involves three of our ten focus cities (Tacoma, Salem, and Eugene). These two state growth-management laws share the common goals of: containing development within defined urban areas; protecting certain types of land such as agricultural, timbered, or environmentally sensitive areas; and expanding infrastructure to meet development (Association of Washington Cities, 1990). Both of these laws authorize some new revenue sources (such as developer impact fees, called "system development charges" in Oregon), and require compliance such as planning at the local level and, in some cases, planning on regional levels.

Another constraint or requirement more commonly imposed on cities by states is a requirement to plan. All ten cities in our study are required by their states to plan. While planning is not in and of itself a growth-management technique, the directing and timing of development is clearly a part of the planning process. When state planning requirements include forced regional planning, the result can be similar to the managing of growth under growth-management laws. As Table 3.2 indicates, six of our ten cities are required to plan in conjunction with other units of government, usually the county. Of the ten cities, eight also make use of the urban growth boundary, or "area of city impact." In some cases,

Table 3.1
Local Growth Management in Ten Urban West Cities

Cities	Low Density Zoning	Building Moratoria	Infrastructure Pacekeeping	Annex Policy	Vote before Development	Neighborhood Groups	Initiative Use	Media Stand on Growth
Reno	N	N	N	Y	N	N	N	N
Pueblo	N	N	N	N	N	N	N	N
Salt Lake	Y[1]	N	Y[2]	Y	N	N	N	N
Boise	N	N	N	N	N	Y[3]	N	N
Tacoma	Y	N	Y[4]	N	N	N	N	Y
Spokane	N	N	N	Y	N	N	N	N
Eugene	Y	N	Y	Y	N	N	Y[5]	Y
Salem	N	N	Y	Y	N	N	N	N
Modesto	N	N	Y	Y	Y[6]	Y[7]	Y[8]	Y
Tempe	N	N	N	Y	N	Y[9]	N	Y

Source: Authors' survey.

Notes:
[1] Salt Lake City has low density zoning as part of its "foothills protection ordinance."
[2] Salt Lake City considers the improvements required of subdividers (roads, sewers, sidewalks, etc.) as "pace-keeping" requirements.
[3] Groups formed to fight development of the Boise foothills.
[4] Via developer impact fees. The same applies for Eugene, Salem, and Modesto.
[5] Initiative concerned with the protection of "historic trees" in reaction to plans to widen city arterials.
[6] Measure A: advisory vote of citizens before sewer trunk line extensions.
[7] G.O.A.L. and Ecology Action Educational Institute are the major groups in Modesto. G.O.A.L. is the group that sponsored Measure A.
[8] Measure A requires an advisory vote of citizens before sewer trunk lines are extended.
[9] Tempe Tomorrow is a group advocating "slower growth" in Tempe.

Table 3.2
State-Level Growth Management in Ten Urban West Cities

Cities	State Growth Manage Law	State Required To Plan	Planning Required with other Units of Government	Urban Growth Boundary
Reno	N	Y	Y	Y[1]
Pueblo	N	Y	N	Y
Salt Lake	N	Y	N	Y
Boise	N	Y	Y	Y
Tacoma	Y	Y	Y	Y
Spokane	N[2]	Y	N	N
Eugene	Y	Y	Y	Y
Salem	Y	Y	Y	Y
Modesto	N	Y	Y	Y
Tempe	N	Y	N	N

Source: Authors' Survey

Notes: [1]Part of regional plan required by the state of Nevada, Reno's UGB has no growth management aspects.
[2]Washington's growth-management law does not at this writing require all counties/cities to participate. Spokane does not.

this is required under state growth-management laws (as in Tacoma); in others it is negotiated between the city and county voluntarily (as in Salt Lake City).

Use of Local Growth-Management Techniques

With the exception of annexation policies, which seven out of ten cities currently use, very few of our ten cities have adopted local growth-management techniques (see Table 3.1). These annexation policies all refer to requiring citizens receiving city services to support annexation to the city in the future. Infrastructure pace-keeping is employed by six cities, although in four municipalities this is accomplished through state-authorized impact fees. Only Salt Lake City and Pueblo reported imposing infrastructure improvement standards that they considered infrastructure pace-keeping measures that were not impact fee based. Modesto is the lone city required to have a vote of the citizenry before development is approved. This is a result of a citizens initiative that requires an advisory vote of the people before new sewer-system trunk lines may be added to the system. None of the ten cities reported using building permit moratoria to control or limit growth.

Use of Local Citizen-Based Growth Management

While several of our cities indicated that they had many neighborhood groups—some of which were initially put into place by city efforts— only Modesto, Boise, and Tempe indicated that they had neighborhood groups that actively opposed growth. The groups in Modesto and Tempe appear to be concerned primarily with slowing the pace of growth, while in Boise these groups are formed around protecting the foothills that surround the city as well as environmentally sensitive areas within the metropolitan Boise area.

Only two cities, Modesto and Eugene, reported that citizens had used the initiative process on the local level to limit or control growth. In Modesto, the neighborhood group Growth, Orderly, Affordable, and Liveable (GOAL) successfully put on the ballot a measure requiring an advisory vote of the citizens before extending the sewer trunk line (Modesto Citizens Advisory Growth Management Act, 1979) (see the case study: Modesto, California—Citizens Respond to Rapid Growth). In Eugene, citizens opposed to the widening of several urban arterials successfully placed on the ballot an initiative protecting historic trees. According to city officials, however, the historic trees question was defeated the first time it was put to the test of the voters (M. D. Gleason, personal communication, 1990).

CASE STUDY: MODESTO, CALIFORNIA—CITIZENS RESPOND TO RAPID GROWTH

Modesto's experience with Measure A, which requires an advisory vote on sewer trunk line extensions, highlights many of the diverse opinions commonly expressed about growth management. Is growth management a necessary tool to prevent the crises of congestion, sprawl, and pollution? Or is it rather a way to scare away jobs and send developments leapfrogging out onto prime agricultural land? These are some of the questions faced by communities contemplating growth management.

The City of Modesto (1990 pop. 164,730) is in the fertile San Joaquin valley of central California. Home to Gallo Wineries, Modesto is surrounded by productive agricultural land and is the location of numerous food and beverage processing industries. Coping with rapid population growth has been an issue in Modesto for decades. From its incorporation in 1884 through 1977, Modesto experienced an average annual growth rate of 4.4 percent. In the period between 1970 and 1976, Modest actually "grew more rapidly than any other California city with a population of 50,000 or more at the time of the 1970 census" (Modesto Planning and Community Development Department, personal communication, 1990). The overall rate of growth in Modesto continues to be high; between 1970 and 1990, for example, the city grew 149 percent, the third-highest growth rate among all thirty-four cities with populations between 100,000 and 200,000 in the eight Western states in our study (see Table 2.5).

Divisions among the citizens of Modesto in regard to the city's expansion in size began to crystallize during the rapid growth of the 1970s. A citizens interest group, GOAL, was formed to give voice to those who feared the consequences of too rapid and uncontrolled growth. According to one of GOAL's founders, Peggy Mensinger (personal communication, July 19, 1990), a former mayor and council member in Modesto, GOAL grew in large part out of the perception that the City Council was unduly influenced by the development community. Taking advantage of the initiative process whereby through the gathering of signatures citizens can place a measure on the ballot for a vote of the electorate, GOAL successfully placed Measure A on the Modesto city election ballot in 1979.

Measure A, the "Modesto Citizens Advisory Growth Management Act," was passed by the narrow margin of 52 percent to 48 percent in 1979 (Modesto Planning and Community Development Department, personal communication, 1990). Measure A requires the following:

> The City Council of the City of Modesto shall not approve, authorize, or appropriate funds for the extension of any sewer trunk without first holding an advisory election as provided by Section 5353 of the California Elections Code. For the purposes of this ordinance, the word "extension" shall mean the addition of sewer trunk capacity to permit expansion of urban development into the Urban Reserve area of the General Plan so as to require amendment of the General Plan, but shall not include any maintenance, repairs, renovation, or improvements to an existing sewer trunk solely for the purposes of safe, efficient, and effective operation thereof. (Modesto Citizens Advisory Growth Management Act, 1979)

Given that the city's sewer system was near capacity, this measure effectively ensured an advisory vote about any new housing or commercial expansions of any size.

The arguments made for and against Measure A by the citizens of Modesto are illustrative of the conflicts inherent in the discussion of nearly all growth-management mechanisms. For many, the issue of growth management involves either a fear of losing the quality of life that brought them to the area because of the problems accompanying rapid growth, or a fear that growth management will result in a loss of jobs and economic vitality. The following excerpts from the ballot measure give voice to these concerns. Writing in opposition to Measure A, Lee Davies, Carl Ulrich, Jr., and Jeff Cowan (1979), identified as members of Modesto for a Better Tomorrow, argued:

> If Measure A is successful many hundreds of jobs could disappear. Affordable housing could become a thing of the past. Costs could rise for industry, and ultimately be paid by us, the consumers. The price tag of Measure A is high. It is asking us to trade jobs, affordable housing and our quality of life for poor planning, more government expenses, higher living costs and unemployment.

Writing on the other side of the argument, Richard T. Harriman and Jon G. H. Shastid (1979) emphasized instead the threat to quality of life that growth represents.

> The price tag of Measure A is low. It asks us only to trade the tremendous profits of a very few for the preservation of the quality of life that brought our families to Modesto to find. Exploitive development is rampant in Modesto. What is happening today in Modesto is exactly what happened to San Jose. . . . Measure A will allow us to pass on to our children their home, intact.

In the late 1980s, Modesto was still experiencing pressures from pro-development interests for continued growth. Of the four advisory votes taken since the adoption of Measure A in 1979, however, only one sewer trunk extension has been approved by the voters (Modesto Planning and Community Development Department, personal communication, 1990). In 1989, the city council, working in conjunction with GOAL and other groups such as the Chamber of Commerce and Ecology Action (another slow-growth group), adopted a new approach to dealing with Modesto's growth future. A comprehensive plan was adopted to allow the growth of villages, which will be multiple-use nuclei of residential and commercial properties. Several villages were planned in sequence, the first having been approved by the electorate (via Measure A) in November 1990. The city anticipates that this will allow well-planned expansion of the housing stock and represent a workable balance between the need to grow and quality of life. In the meantime, people are continuing to discover the affordable housing and pleasant atmosphere that Modesto has to offer. The most recent waves of newcomers are buying affordable homes in Modesto and commuting the seventy to ninety miles to the Bay area each day.

CONCLUSION

Beliefs about how much growth is good and what kinds of growth are desirable in a community are tied to the vision of the city held by its officials and citizens. When competing visions of a city's future shape and character clash, there is conflict. Even when there is consensus about growth, pursuing the particular vision chosen proves to be very difficult because growth turns out to be the cumulative result of many forces— some at cross-purposes, others producing unexpected synergies—few of which are under the control of City Hall. National and international economic conditions prompt businesses to move or stay, close or thrive. People move from community to community, some seeking jobs, others seeking quality of life. Paradoxically, the same city is a growth "boom town" to some new residents, and a quality-of-life haven for others. These competing visions are reflected in the case study of Boise.

The ability of a city to steer a particular course in regard to growth is restricted. As the chapter outlined, many other actors define when and how growth will be handled in cities. Growth management, for example, must be understood within the intergovernmental context. The package of policies available to cities to manage growth is the result of state laws and restrictions, county actions, and, sometimes, citizen initiatives. Our review of growth-management techniques in our ten focus cities indicates that only a few of the ten cities are utilizing growth controls that originated through city government action alone. For example, only two cities reported using low-density zoning, and one of the Urban West municipalities is using building permit stoppages (see Table 3.1). Many, if not most, of the growth-limiting policies we examined in this chapter originated either with the states or the citizens. That is to say, the cities have had these growth-limiting policies imposed on them. Steering a course with growth is further compounded by the fact that beyond the intergovernmental constraints, growth-management techniques in general appear to be an unwieldy tool. Studies indicate that their ability to slow growth is modest (Leutwiler, 1987; Logan and Zhou, 1989). The situation is equally difficult for cities seeking growth, as studies show that commonly used tax incentives have only a modest ability to attract new business (see Smith, Ready, and Judd [1992] for a review of these studies; also see Swanstrom [1989]).

The differing perspectives taken on growth by Urban West cities were illustrated by our case studies, in which communities struggled to find the proper balance between growth (and jobs?) and quality of life (limits to growth?). Is growth a curse or golden opportunity? The answer to this depends on one's perspective, explaining in part why growth and growth-management problems remain two of the most volatile issues faced by local governments.

NOTES

1. We do not include a full discussion of the use of various metropolitan reforms here as growth-management tools in part because such proposals are so seldom approved by voters. This does not mean, however, that proposals for reforms such as consolidation of city and county governments are not under discussion. The Spokane area continues to consider city–county consolidation among other options (see Witt, Steger, Pierce, and Lovrich [1989]), and discussion of consolidation of services continues in Boise and Salt Lake City. For a review of the success and failure of metropolitan reforms see Vincent L. Marando (1979: 409–421).

2. Public hearings for annexation purposes are not always taken seriously by city officials. One city official, who will remain anonymous, told a student researcher, "We call [citizens in proposed annexation area] in, listen to what they have to say, and then annex them anyway" (Gibson, 1992:3).

4

Infrastructure

This chapter considers the many pressures on municipal infrastructures due to increased growth, changes in federal funding, and revenue limitations imposed by local voters. This chapter also illustrates how some cities plan infrastructure improvements and coordinate their physical and financial planning. The importance of capital budgeting and the role of capital improvement plans in growing cities will be analyzed.

At the outset, it is important to consider the many dimensions of the term "infrastructure" as it relates to municipal affairs. The term generally refers to the system of physical structures necessary to sustain the operation of cities—roads, bridges, sewer and water treatment plants, city halls, and fire stations. But infrastructure means more than just bricks and mortar. The concept of infrastructure carries economic, public service, and quality-of-life implications. A statement in the *New Mexico Capital Improvements Programming Manual* aptly describes the meaning of the term in its broader sense. "The term 'infrastructure' is used widely to describe the collection of public works that are essential to support economic activity, and promote a desirable quality of life" (Butler and Reed, 1990:1).

Consideration of infrastructure issues in this study is important not only because of their relationship to growth, but also because of the enormous costs associated with infrastructure investment. Some of the characteristics of infrastructure illustrate the serious fiscal challenges communities face in trying to maintain or upgrade their facilities. An infrastructure facility is typically capital-intensive, has a long life, and has high operation and maintenance costs (Apogee Research, 1987).

INFRASTRUCTURE ISSUES DURING THE 1980s

According to an analysis done by the Chicago Federal Reserve Bank, infrastructure investment in the United States has dropped steadily since 1963 (Butler and Reed, 1990). It is beyond the scope of our study to examine all of the factors that contributed to this situation; however, it is important to point out that throughout the decade 1978–1988, infrastructure issues were important items on the public agenda. Infrastructure failures were discussed in the academic literature, in reports commissioned by governmental entities, and in the popular media. The infrastructure crisis was featured in such popular news magazines as *Time, Business Week, Newsweek,* and *U.S. News and World Report.* Dramatic stories detailing the collapse of bridges, water systems, and other infrastructure components caught the national attention—at least for a time.

A report from the Joint Economic Committee of the U.S. Congress commented on the decline in capital spending and expressed the view that this lack of investment was "the single greatest problem facing our nation's cities" (Urban Land Institute, 1989: iii). Pat Choate and Susan Walter (1989), in their publication, *America in Ruins,* noted that the crisis or ruin in which the nation's infrastructure existed would be a "critical bottleneck to the national economic renewal" (cited in Urban Land Institute, 1989:xi).

The need for increased spending on America's infrastructure was well documented. Numerous studies have detailed the declining rates of spending for infrastructure and infrastructure maintenance. The National Council on Public Works Improvement (1988: 20) concluded after its two-year investigation of the condition of American Public Works that "the current level of capital investment is barely enough to offset annual depreciation, much less meet new demands." The dollar figures attached to these analyses of America's infrastructure needs were staggering. The interstate highway system was estimated to need $33 billion in repairs in the 1980s, and primary and secondary roads were estimated to require over $500 billion worth of investment just to keep them in their current deteriorated condition (Barker, 1984). A summary of a 1991 Federal Highway Administration report notes that, even with aggressive congestion-management programs, the cost of improving pavement conditions and reducing congestion will mean an annual investment of $60 billion to $80 billion a year for the next twenty years, about triple the nation's current investment in highways. Maintaining current conditions would cost $33.1 billion a year or twice current spending levels ("On the Road Again," 1992).

Idaho, with only a million residents, was estimated to require nearly $7.3 billion to address the most urgent needs of the state's local transportation system (maintenance), a figure many times the state's annual general fund (Wilber Smith Associates et al., 1990). Oregon, meanwhile, estimated its backlog at $6 billion required to bring roads and bridges to a modest standard for pavement condition, capacity, and design (Price Waterhouse, 1986).

All such infrastructure studies seem to have uncovered a great deal of impressive evidence concerning the enormous investment needed to address the poor condition of the nation's infrastructure. These studies were in agreement that the serious underinvestment in infrastructure is a major drag on the nation's economic potential. Although disagreement exists as to the cost associated with the infrastructure problem, there is general consensus that the cost will be high by any standard.

Students of infrastructure issues also agreed that the nation's transportation infrastructure (roads, streets, and bridges) had the most critical repair and replacement needs. According to an Urban Land Institute (1989) overview of infrastructure needs-assessment studies, the nation's transportation infrastructure needs ranged between two-thirds to three-fourths of all of the projected costs of dealing with the country's basic infrastructure needs.

As noted earlier, cities face the challenge of maintaining and expanding their transportation systems at a time in which federal aid, once plentiful, is drying up and citizens have become increasingly resistant to raising taxes. A number of studies indicate that when faced with revenue shortfalls, cities tend to reduce spending on capital projects in order to continue current levels of support for more visible operations (Pagano, 1988). Even though this is the general trend among cities nationally, it is interesting to note the variations among Urban West cities. (See Table 4.1 for a breakdown of the percentage of total budgets committed to capital-outlay expenditures among the Urban West cities.) The same would seem to be true of states and counties. One county commissioner interviewed as part of this study remarked that when faced with a trade-off between laying off employees or fudging on capital projects, local governments fudge on the capital projects.

URBAN WEST INFRASTRUCTURE NEEDS

Several Urban West cities report that spending on capital projects had to be deferred because of declining revenue. In Modesto, California, "before the passage of Proposition 13 in June, 1978, the city was able to

Table 4.1
Capital Outlay as a Percentage of Total Budgeted Expenditures among Urban West Cities

CITIES	1982	1984	1987
Glendale	40	21	30
Tempe	37	24	39
Bakersfield	12	15	16
Berkeley	5	5	10
Chula Vista	11	44	18
Concord	17	38	24
Fremont	32	57	16
Fullerton	22	22	19
Garden Grove	21	24	5
Glendale	28	22	26
Hayward	26	18	11
Huntington Beach	14	18	4
Inglewood	9	16	4
Lakewood	24	42	4
Modesto	25	19	29
Ontario	11	27	11
Orange	14	11	33

devote half of the sales tax revenue received ... to needed capital improvements. Afterwards, this Council policy was gradually abandoned in an effort to help finance the cost of ongoing department operations" (Lipsky, 1990: ii). The City of Salem, Oregon, reports that there has been a 63 percent reduction in the funding available for asphalt overlay since 1980, and that "pavement and bridge maintenance have been deferred" (Mauldin, 1990:1). (See the case study: "Salem, Oregon—Confronting the Costs.") Other cities struggle to cope with reductions in federal funds once targeted for capital expenses by shifting the burden to other sectors of the budget. Eugene, Oregon, City Manager Michael Gleason (1990), wrote that

Table 4.1 (continued)

CITIES	1982	1984	1987
Oxnard	8	12	22
Pasadena	15	23	6
Pomona	7	54	9
Riverside	26	25	20
San Bernadino	8	28	20
Stockton	15	15	12
Sunnyvale	23	25	12
Torrance	11	11	9
Pueblo	17	25	9
Boise	22	25	22
Las Vegas	5	19	6
Reno	15	22	41
Eugene	29	21	11
Salem	17	28	3
Salt Lake City	24	33	33
Spokane	23	18	18
Tacoma	38	15	22

Source: The Municipal Yearbook, 1984, 1987, 1990.

the capital budget continues to receive General Fund support comparable to the level previously funded through Federal Revenue
Sharing as part of Council's effort to increase the support to infrastructure maintenance and rehabilitation. As you recall, Federal
Revenue Sharing funds had been dedicated by Council to finance
General Capital projects. Loss of this funding source has placed an
additional burden on local resources. (p. iii)

Eugene and other cities also seek to fund transportation infrastructure
with innovative and creative approaches such as developer-paid impact
fees, use of special assessment districts, and cooperative intergovernmental agreements. The characteristic that all of these revenue innovations share, of course, is their ability to provide new revenue streams to

cities outside of the traditional property tax. Given the new limitations faced by most cities in the 1980s (see chapter 2), these alternatives become extremely valuable sources of municipal finance. These innovations are discussed in greater detail in the next chapter.

CASE STUDY: SALEM, OREGON—CONFRONTING THE COSTS

As noted in the introduction to this chapter, cities across the country have been confronting the fact that our nation's transportation infrastructure is in a seriously deteriorated condition. The costs associated with repairing and maintaining our existing system of roads and bridges by all accounts are staggering. Many cities have tried to deal with growing fiscal shortages by cutting back on expenditures for roadway repair and maintenance. When cities face tradeoffs between highly demanded services such as keeping a law enforcement officer on the beat or funding street maintenance fully, it is often the infrastructure maintenance and repair that are deferred. Salem, Oregon, is typical of many cities confronting the staggering costs of maintaining and repairing the elements of their transportation infrastructures.

Salem (1990 population, 107,786) is approximately sixty miles south of Portland on the banks of the Willamette River. Salem has grown steadily since 1970 (1970 population, 69,725), and has had an 8.5 percent growth in population in the period of 1980–1988 (Division of Economic and Community Development, 1990). As the state capital, Salem has almost 30 percent of its employment in the governmental sector, although food processing and manufacturing industries are also important to Salem's economy (Division of Economic and Community Development, 1990).

Paying for infrastructure is cited as a hardship by most cities, and Salem is certainly no exception. Oregon cities have faced the double disadvantage of operating under a property tax limitation and having a state system without a sales tax. The existing property tax limitation was recently made to look luxurious by the passage of Measure 5, a new and much stricter property tax limitation approved by voters in the fall 1990 election. The earlier limits to revenue generation had in small part been addressed by a state land-use law that allowed cities to charge impact fees (called system development charges) to help development pay as the city grows.

Conflict over impact fees was high in Salem during the decade. City officials report that the impact fees put in place in the late 1970s were rolled back in the 1980s due to intense resistance from the development community and fear that the high rates were causing new projects to fail (Eide, Ingraham, and Wacker, personal communication, July 8, 1990). City staff lament the loss of the revenue while developers feel the remaining fees are destructive. Interviews revealed the animosity that can surround this issue. A high-ranking city staff member stated, "It's hard to fight people who want to screw the future to make money today." And a leader in the development community said, "City staffers are ivory tower people who don't know anything about how the world works."

The city began to assess the amount of revenue that would be needed to repair and maintain its street systems at various levels of quality by researching and producing a report, "Street Maintenance Cost of Service Analysis." This report details a background of declining spending on street maintenance and repair. For instance, in the period between 1979 and 1990 there was a 38 percent reduction in the number of street maintenance workers, a 63 percent reduction in the amount of contract asphalt overlay work done each year, and a deferral of bridge maintenance (Salem Public Works Department, 1990).

The city's Public Works Department estimated that in 1990, it would cost $200 million to maintain Salem's streets at half the recommended maintenance over the next ten years (F. Mauldin, personal communication, July 9, 1990). This price tag assumes no growth and no new federal mandates, both unlikely assumptions. The maintenance cycle for Salem's streets is estimated at an incredible 180 years. The preferred maintenance cycle is forty years for a residential street, thirty for collectors, and twenty for arterials (Eide et al., personal communication, 1990).

A $200 million price tag would be staggering under any circumstances, but Salem faces this projected cost while laboring under Measure 5. This voter-approved constitutional change limits the total nonschool property tax assessments to $10 per $1,000 of assessed market value. For the City of Salem, this represents a tremendous cut in existing revenue. Confronting the cost of infrastructure has become more challenging than ever for city officials in Oregon's capital.

Infrastructure Financing Issues

The funding for municipal infrastructure traditionally has come from three basic sources: borrowing, current revenue, and intergovernmental aid. Federal and state aid have been major sources of infrastructure financing, especially in highways, wastewater treatment, transit, and community development. Many improvements in local government infrastructure were primarily funded by federal grants. The impact of these grants was not always positive, however. According to J. E. Peterson (1988), the availability of certain grants has influenced the type of infrastructure improvements made in many communities. Grants made available with low matching-funds requirements unduly influenced some local infrastructure decisions. Projects were too often undertaken because of the availability of funds as opposed to their inherent merit.

Wastewater treatment plants were too often constructed of far greater capacity than many communities needed. Such overbuilding was a classic example on the waste in federal resources. Federal grants also had a substitution impact on local government spending. Local revenue that might have been made available for infrastructure financing was diverted to other uses when federal funds were made available. Because of concerns about such questionable spending practices, combined with the move to reduce the federal deficit, many of the federal programs for infrastructure development and maintenance were cut or eliminated. In their place, especially in the environmental area, have emerged state revolving-loan programs.

Current municipal income from cities' own sources of revenue has been an additional, though limited, source of funding. This is the more conservative pay-as-you-go approach that most rapidly growing communities do not have the luxury to rely on to any significant degree. Typically, large amounts of own-source revenue are not available, largely because it is difficult to generate the amount of money needed or to assert the kind of political discipline needed to accumulate funds and resist the temptation to divert such earmarked dollars for operating budget purposes. However, there is one area in which own-source revenue is significant. The funding of lease-purchase agreements from own-source revenue is becoming increasingly popular, particularly since they do not have to undergo the rigors and risks of a bond election (J. E. Peterson, 1988). Local voter resistance to most tax increases makes this a popular alternative.

Borrowing for long-term purposes generates major amounts of money for improvements from either general obligation or revenue bonds (see chapter 5 for a more complete discussion). Borrowing was the most important form of financing in the 1950s and is again becoming a major source of financing. Whether or not this will continue to be a major source may be decided by federal legislative initiatives or federal judicial decisions limiting the tax-exempt status of many municipal bonds (see chapter 5).

Federal tax reform in 1986 tightened the requirements for tax-exempt bonds, making distinctions between government and private activity bonds. Many bonds utilized for private activity purposes either have lost or will lose their tax-exempt status. The major effect on local government is, of course, that higher interest rates would be charged local governments by having to rely on taxable bonds.

Recent U.S. Supreme Court decisions have also had potentially devastating impacts on local government borrowing authority. The *South Carolina v. Baker, Treasury Secretary of the U.S.* (1988) decision removed the prohibition that barred the national government from eliminating the tax-exempt status of municipal bonds. If taxes were imposed on municipal bonds, city leaders would view this as a violation of the concept of intergovernmental tax immunity and could have major negative consequences on the capacity of local governments to fund infrastructure improvements. The price tag for redeeming municipal bonds could rise considerably.

The relationship among these various sources of infrastructure revenue and their contribution to infrastructure investment has significantly changed over the past several decades. During the decade of the 1950s, there was considerable emphasis on highway spending, and many transportation improvements were financed by long-term debt. During the 1960s, conservation and water systems received substantially greater attention. Debt financing declined but federal aid became more of a factor, and local government entities began to fund some of their improvements out of user charges. In the decade of the 1970s, infrastructure spending began to decline, except for sewer construction. Spending for sewers was substantially aided by federal assistance. Funding from user charges declined, however. Spending during this period was restrained by the negative impacts of inflation, federal cutbacks, and some property tax limitations (Paul Peterson, 1981). To get a better understanding of the specific types of infrastructure policies adopted by cities, we now turn to the expenditure and revenue practices developed by our Urban West focus cities.

Revenue and Expenditure among Urban West Focus Cities

Utilizing biannual census data, Table 4.2 displays the per capita spending of the Urban West cities on highways from 1977 through 1987. The average per capita expenditure for highways among the Urban West cities is $71. The U.S. average per capita expenditure on highways in fiscal year 1987 was $214 (U.S. Advisory Commission on Intergovernmental Relations, 1987: Table 53). The highest average per capita expenditure over the decade (1976–1987) on highways was $122 in Salt Lake City. The lowest average per capita expenditure for this decade was in Pueblo, with a level of $37.90. It should be noted, however, that many cities had significant variation in their per capita spending over the 1977–1987 period. Reno, for example, following the passage of a major bond issue for roads, had a tremendous jump in spending from $49.76 per capita in 1985–1986 to $127.77 in 1986–1987. A similar pattern in highway spending holds for Tempe, which had a 1985–1986 per capita expenditure of $70.83, and $138.41 in 1986–1987. Although several cities had their highest level of per capita spending in the mid-1980s (see Salt Lake City, Eugene, and Salem, for example), only Pueblo ended the 1977–1987 decade with a lower level of per capita spending ($23.76) than it began with

Table 4.2
Per Capita Highway Expenditure Trends for Ten Urban West Focus Cities,
1977–1987

Cities	1976-1977	1981-1982	1982-1983	1984-1985	1985-1986	1986-1987	Mean
Spokane	20.92	53.49	67.22	67.5	66.76	63.99	56.64
Tacoma	85.37	83.65	64.13	89.38	111.11	102.92	89.4
Salt Lake	39.18	106.83	101.11	183.16	163.17	141.07	122.42
Pueblo	27.8	43.67	81.3	50.34	20.83	23.76	37.9
Reno	43.64	38.06	41.35	42.2	49.76	127.77	57.13
Modesto	30.42	47.08	46.78	54.36	46.43	61.44	48.5
Tempe	23.03	54.1	62.86	70.72	70.83	138.41	69.9
Eugene	32.86	112.07	96.71	140.03	73.04	54.14	86.47
Salem	78.09	74.89	54.74	73.05	86.95	79.3	74.63

Source: U.S. Bureau of the Census

($27.80). Pueblo also had the lowest mean level of per capita spending
for the decade ($37.90).

Revenue Sources for Transportation Expenditures

As described in the prior section, most cities have had to adapt to the
changes in the fiscal environment by shifting expenditures to new revenue sources or finding new funding mechanisms. Table 4.3 displays the
various sources of transportation revenue for the Urban West cities. As
Tables 4.3 and 4.4 indicate, there is wide variation among the study cities
in regard to their sources of transportation revenue. While cities, such
as Boise and Salem remain substantially dependent on the property tax
(which mimics the overall state reliance on the property tax in Oregon
and Idaho, as was discussed in chapter 2), other cities such as Modesto
and Tempe have virtually no reliance on the property tax and show a
greater diversity in the number of revenue sources available to them. In
some cases, this reflects more taxation and revenue authorities given by
the state government.

MUNICIPAL BUDGETING PROCESS AND
INFRASTRUCTURE

Historically, the operating budget that funds the city's visible services
attracts the most attention and the most dollars. Public safety, parks and

Table 4.3
Local Revenue for Transportation for Selected Urban West Focus Cities

Cities	Property Tax	LID	Excise Taxes	Charge Permits	Gen Fund	Local Option Taxes	Traffic Fines	Other Local Govern	Impact Fees	Fund Bal	Bonds & Notes	Private Contrib
Tacoma	.02	.15	.01*	.004	.34			.007**				
Spokane	.07	.05		.03	.30						.03	.002
Eugene	.14				.04			.06***	.03	.04	.47	.006
Salem	.30	.01			.06		.004		.004	.29		.002
Modesto							.12		****			
Boise	.37											
Pueblo	.04	.09			.06		.08	.04				
Tempe										.02	.41*****	

Sources: Washington Department of Transportation, "City/Town Report to the Secretary of Transportation for Budget Year 1989"; Oregon Department of Transportation, "Survey of Local Road and Street Finances for Year Ended June 30, 1989"; Modesto, "Proposed City Budget 1990-91"; Ada County Highway District, "1988-89 Annual Report"; Pueblo, "Comprehensive Annual Financial Report for Year Ended December 31, 1989"; and Tempe, "City Budget 1990-91."

Notes: Numbers are percentages of total revenue and may not add to 1.0 due to rounding errors.
* Mobile home excise tax.
** Reimbursement from sewer utility.
*** Includes money from intergovernmental agreement between Eugene and Land County (see Urban Transition Agreement).
**** The city of Modesto anticipates $4,000,000 from impact fees in 1990-91.
***** Tempe has established a tax increment mechanism to fund improvements out of its enterprise fund.

Table 4.4
State and Other Sources of Revenue for Transportation for Selected Urban West Focus Cities

Cities	State					Federal	Other
	Highway User Fund	Sales Tax	Grants	Other/ General	Lottery		
Tacoma	.25		.002	.03		.03	.15
Spokane	.13		.02			.09	.30
Eugene	.16			.008			.04
Salem	.21					.02	.10
Modesto	.88						
Boise	.34	.02				.12	.15
Pueblo	.39			.06		.08	.15
Tempe	.54				.03		

Sources: Washington Department of Transportation, "City/Town Report to the Secretary of Transportation for Budget Year 1989"; Oregon Department of Transportation, "Survey of Local Road and Street Finances for Year Ended June 30, 1989"; Modesto, "Proposed City Budget 1990-91"; Ada County Highway District, "1988-89 Annual Report"; Pueblo, "Comprehensive Annual Financial Report for Year Ended December 31, 1989"; and Tempe, "City Budget 1990-91."

Note: Numbers are percentages of total revenue and may not add to 1.0 due to rounding errors.

recreation, and other programs that people readily identify as traditional city services are the focus of most budget discussions. However, most of the infrastructure components, the city's "invisible" services, have typically received less attention. The infrastructure components are invisible in that they rarely come to mind unless they are not working. For these and other reasons, infrastructure needs have been historically ignored until they threaten the health or growth potential of a city, as they appeared to do in the 1980s. Studies documenting the deterioration of these systems seem to have little lasting impact, and needs assessments showing the staggering price tags needed to repair such systems have little meaning to the average citizen until the systems break down or the future health and growth of the community are threatened by their collapse.

Successful infrastructure planning requires a commitment by the governing body to educate and involve the public in understanding the importance of and making decisions about infrastructure investment. Commitment from elected officials is also critical to implementing whatever final decisions are made, directing city staff to gather the necessary information, and encouraging public input.

Infrastructure planning requires cities to undertake and maintain a comprehensive inventory and evaluation of existing public facilities. This activity gives city officials a better understanding of the value of their systems and what it will take to address any discovered deficiencies. Most of the Urban West focus cities have undertaken such analyses of the condition of their transportation systems. Reno, for example, has done a systematic assessment of the pavement maintenance and repair needs of its city streets. Although the average street in Reno was found to be in relatively good condition, city officials documented a backlog of repair and reconstruction needs that exceeded $36 million. If current street funding levels were to continue, they believe that by the fiscal year 1998–1999 their backlog would exceed $134 million (S. Varela, personal communication to G. Etcherey, February 27, 1990).

Effective infrastructure planning requires an appreciation of the difficulties in defining crucial concepts like deficiency and adequacy, given the fact that service standards and public facility-performance ratings are ultimately shaped by value or political judgments. In short, city officials have to determine what criteria they will use to measure where they are today and where they want to be in the future in regard to infrastructure planning. Establishing as a matter of policy that the status quo is adequate, or determining the acceptable level of service standards, is crucial in infrastructure planning. The service standard level the city wants to maintain in the number of acres of parks per person, number of fire stations per capita, or level of classification of city streets is an important planning consideration.

Long-range and infrastructure planning requires that growing cities estimate what their future service demands will be and who will create those additional demands. They have to answer such questions as: How much will be created by proposed new developments? How much will be created by existing residents and businesses desiring new levels of services? What will the future look like in the way of additional people and new housing stock? What kinds of services will these new people and facilities require?

There are a number of fiscal-impact models cities use to make their revenue and expenditure projections. The appropriateness of the models varies depending on the socioeconomic and geographic circumstances of a given city. The correct model can provide an important road map for cities in determining where gaps might occur between expected revenue and expenditures for infrastructure. The development of this information is critical to determining what anticipated costs should be funded by what revenue source (Burchell and Listokin, 1980).

Regardless of which model is used, however, forecasting revenue is complicated by the unstable or unpredictable nature of some municipal revenue sources. The major source of revenue for most city services is the property tax, even for such infrastructure components as streets, bridges, and fire stations. Even though the property tax is noted for its stability and its productivity, its use is not always within the control of city officials. It can be limited, as in some of our Urban West cities, by citizens' initiatives or state laws. The health of the city tax base can also be a consideration. Overly optimistic projections of property tax-valuation increases can create revenue shortfall problems. Intergovernmental aid in the form of federal and state grants or revenue sharing can fluctuate considerably, depending on state or federal legislative or congressional action. The city should also take into account the development of alternative revenue sources that might be developed and the policy of bonded indebtedness that might be pursued to provide the up-front capital needed to finance public facilities required by growth.

Another consideration is the action of other governmental entities and how their policies might affect the future growth and development of the city. Different types of governmental entities are responsible for different types of infrastructures. Transportation infrastructure is an example in which, for both funding and administrative purposes, the federal, state, and local governments are involved in varying ways. The city looks to the federal and state governments for funding, but also has to be concerned about the county or highway district plans for streets and bridges in the urban fringe areas.

Related to the budgeting process involving revenue and expenditure forecasting is the capital improvement plan (CIP). Capital improvement plans and capital budgets are related in that the plan "identifies the improvements and the capital budget allocates the money" (Butler and Reed, 1990:6). Capital improvement plans assist communities in making fundamental decisions about the speed and direction of growth in their communities. Basic community decisions are reflected in these important documents. In this process, choices are made about the need for constructing various types of facilities and how the construction of each will help address community needs and interests. The magnitude and direction of growth of the community can be influenced greatly by the placement of public facilities such as streets, schools, fire stations, and so on.

The capital improvement plan is the traditional tool for planning infrastructure and is a component in most comprehensive plans. In the CIP, cities develop schedules for improvements, define how those improvements will be funded, and identify each project's revenue source. CIPs are not panaceas for the infrastructure financing problem in and of themselves, but they are valuable tools to help cities avoid serious infrastructure deficiencies and plug the gaps between needed revenues to fund growing infrastructure expenditures. Of our Urban West focus cities, Tempe has perhaps the most exemplary plan and implementation track record (see the Tempe case study). At the end of the Urban West decade, Tempe had no major deficiencies in its infrastructure. The city has a well-established capital improvement-planning process, with a recognized city document and a leadership team committed to funding the plan. Because elected officials have committed themselves to this plan, Tempe has demonstrated an awareness that many other cities do not have about the importance of investing in its infrastructure and avoiding the escalating cost of deferring maintenance. In Tempe, the operating budget is important, but it does not totally dominate budgetary considerations.

CASE STUDY: TEMPE, ARIZONA—MAINTAINING A
HUMAN SCALE IN A METROPOLITAN AREA

Once a sleepy college town with agrarian roots, Tempe now lays claim to being the "hub city" of Arizona's Valley of the Sun. Tempe's growth rate has been impressive, from a city of 24,897 in 1960 to 141,865 in 1990. Tempe's "hub" designation is earned through its close proximity to Phoenix's Sky Harbor International Airport, which is ten minutes from the downtown area. It is also the home of Arizona State University, the Phoenix Cardinals (professional football), the Fiesta Bowl (college football), Seattle Mariners' spring training camp (professional baseball), and forty-six industrial parks.

Tempe is landlocked. It is surrounded by Phoenix on the west, Mesa to the east, Chandler on its southern border, and Scottsdale and the Salt River bed to the north. Despite this landlocked situation, Tempe is not merely a metropolitan bedroom community. It is "a rare commodity in metropolitan Phoenix," according to a *Phoenix Gazette* columnist. It has kept its "small town flavor. . . . Tempe has become . . . a true urban village. It has the qualities of a place that is urban, yet it looks and feels like a small town" (Spratt, 1989:A-3).

There has been an impressive continuity in municipal leadership over a twenty-year period as well as a shared vision that evolved over this same period relating to the growth and development of this community, according to Tempe City Manager Terry Zerkle (personal communication, August 1990). Growth-management principles and quality-of-life considerations are important in Tempe. According to a report from the Morrison Institute for Public Policy (1990:40) at Arizona State University, "Tempe is considered a model among Valley cities for its emphasis on quality development that incorporates a high level of aesthetic and environmental considerations. As a result, Tempe successfully has enhanced its physical appeal and can boast of having created a unique, identifiable image."

Unlike most of its neighboring cities and its counterparts in the Urban West, Tempe has not used annexation as a tool to promote growth. Very little of its growth can be attributed to annexation. In the 1970s the city

consciously chose as a matter of policy not to follow the aggressive annexation policies of its neighbors (Foster, 1989). Consequently, Tempe is
almost fully developed but has not sprawled out. Its landlocked position
is both a negative and a positive, depending upon one's perspective. It
is a negative from the standpoint of major new growth initiatives. Less
than 20 percent of the city's land is undeveloped. On the positive side,
however, the city "has turned its attention away from new developing
to preserving and upgrading existing neighborhoods" (Tseffos, 1988: B-
1). Rob Melnick (1989), director of the Morrison Institute at Arizona State
University, believes that the city's landlocked position is a plus. He told
the *Phoenix Gazette*: "Tempe has had to focus on . . . improving the quality of what exists rather than expanding outward. A lot of cities have
been hurt because they gobbled up land all around them. When there
was growth fever and everyone was pushing outward, a lot of cities were
making commitments to the future with developers who now have gone
belly up" (cited in Garcia, 1987:A-10).

Its limited-growth policy has, according to a 1989 survey, made Tempe
the least expensive city in which to live in the Valley. According to an
assistant city manager, "Tempe has limited its growth, and that has
made us a more efficient place to operate. That's reflected in the lower
costs" (DeBruin, 1989:A-1). It has also allowed the city to concentrate on
maintaining and upgrading its infrastructure. There simply are no major
infrastructure problems in Tempe as there are in virtually every other
Urban West city. "At the same time that Tempe was growing," according
to Manager Zerkle (1989), "the city was also putting into place its infrastructure. So it's not a matter of having to go back with great expenditure
for infrastructure after the fact" (cited in Garcia, A-10), which is what
some cities have had to do that have developed aggressive annexation
policies.

Tempe is a model city from the standpoint of having a coherent capital-improvement program with strong elected officials and general public support. In fiscal year 1990, the capital budget constituted over 20
percent of the total budget. The capital-improvement plan is a five-year
plan that is reviewed and adopted annually. Capital projects scheduled
for the upcoming fiscal year are financed from next year's budget, with
the other four years subject to further review and modification in sub-
sequent years. Funds supporting the capital budget come from a variety
of sources. General obligation bond funds provide 28 percent, while the
rest comes from capital reserves and current operating revenues (City of
Tempe, 1990).

Citizen support for general obligation bond financing has been overwhelming. Bond elections have been held every five years since 1970,
and in each election the bond proposals have received overwhelming
public support. The city's debt-management program, which includes

bond financing, is a rather interesting program. The city contracted with the Government Finance Research Center (1989:1) to do a study of "the city's present and future debt capacity." The study was also designed to get a better understanding of how the city's debt compares with those of similar cities and how it could improve its credit position.

Based on this study, the city has developed a long-range debt-management plan and a mechanism to update it based on "population factors, tax base growth and current levels of general operating costs" (City of Tempe, 1990:6). The city has also implemented an innovative tax-increment financing approach whereby water and wastewater treatment bond funds, which are repaid by user fees, are loaned to the capital budget to "finance other capital projects for economic development purposes" (p. 3). The city then pays back the loans through "increased sales taxes generated from area properties" that have benefited from the capital improvements (p. 4). The city was rewarded for its actions with a bond rating increase to AA (Boas, 1990).

CONCLUSION

The infrastructure crisis did not begin during the Urban West decade, but the "realization of the dimensions of the problems reached new heights" at that time (Shirey, 1982:52). Public awareness was raised by national news media that focused on the poor condition of our infrastructure. Stories of infrastructure failure were chronicled in *Time* and other popular news magazines. These stories resonated throughout the country because of a number of factors. The most important from the national perspective was the need to spur a national economic recovery. Infrastructure was recognized for what it was: "the underpinnings of our economic and governmental system" (Shirey, 1982:52) and the "basic framework for growth" (Catanese, 1988:81). The drive for economic recovery, however, was accompanied by reductions in federal funding for infrastructure, increased unfunded mandates on cities, judicial limitation on municipal bonded indebtedness, and revenue limitations imposed by citizen initiatives or by state legislation. In this context, cities were largely left to their own devices to find innovative financing mechanisms to maintain or extend infrastructure. As noted by Choate and Walter, this was a difficult period.

> One-half of the nation's communities cannot allow existing firms to expand or new plants to locate in their borders because water and sewer facilities are operating at or near capacity. Another one-fourth of all communities are unable to improve their economic base because other public facilities such as roads, streets, and waste

disposal sites are either worn out, obsolete, or beyond capacity. (cited in Shirey, 1982:52)

Despite the impacts of external forces on cities, however, our case study of Tempe points out that there is much that a community can do to prepare for growth. This chapter highlighted the need for infrastructure planning and coordination among city departments as well as among governmental entities. Cities that utilize infrastructure planning and a capital budgeting process are in a stronger position to guide their growth rather than reacting on an ad hoc basis to every proposed development. As indicated in Table 4.1, the degree to which Urban West cities invested in their infrastructure varied widely, as has, to a degree, their growth rates. Aggregate national investment data indicate a decline, but that does not mean that all Urban West cities have followed that pattern, as demonstrated in the Tempe case study.

The next chapter discusses in more detail the financing and equity issues relating to increased infrastructure demands and other service requirements in our growing cities. We also comment on the challenges cities face in their search for alternative revenue sources and the limitations placed on their traditional revenue sources.

5

Innovations in Coping with Capital Fiscal Problems

GROWTH IMPACTS

Challenge to Fund Growth-Affected Services

As detailed in chapter 4, the costs of maintaining and improving infrastructure can be staggering. Growth in a city can complicate the already highly difficult task of maintaining infrastructure, as pressure mounts to build needed new roads and public facilities rather than allocate funds to maintain existing ones. As also noted in chapter 4, capital expenditures are difficult for most cities because the costs of infrastructure are "lumpy"—that is, they require large expenditures up front. This chapter will explain some of the changes that have made financing infrastructure maintenance and development more difficult in recent years, and describe some new methods of financing being used by cities to help pay for capital projects.

Over the last decade, three changes in the political and fiscal environment have combined to make financing infrastructure more difficult. The first change in conditions involves the general decline in the number and types of federal grants available to cities for funding municipal infrastructure. The second change entails the consequences of the often severe restrictions placed on city revenue sources by state law. These two developments have been discussed in some detail in chapter 2. The final change to be discussed in this chapter pertains to modifications in the federal tax code that changed the way in which cities could use general obligation and revenue bonds to finance the debt necessary for the maintenance and development of infrastructure facilities and projects.

One of the major issues facing officials in growing communities today is, Who should pay for all this growth? The solution in an increasing number of cities is that growth should pay its own way. Throughout most of our history, growth was assumed to be of such benefit that this issue would never have been seriously discussed. Beginning in the late 1960s, however, the apparent benefits of growth were seriously challenged. The emergence of the environmental movement in this period, among other things, encouraged more public focus on the negative aspects of growth, which "caused pollution, congestion of streets, overuse of community services, increased crime and generally lowered the quality of life" (Nelson, 1988:xxv–xxvi). Other municipal voices also questioned some of the presumed economic benefits of growth, asking whether it generated enough additional revenue to offset its real service impact.

Paying for the costs of growth raises a number of issues for local policy makers. Those who should pay for the impact of growth could be one or more of several types of groups. New residents are expected to pay for some of the service and facility costs they create, but should they be held responsible for all growth-related costs, even though every resident benefits to some degree from growth? Furthermore, current residents will benefit to some degree from the new facilities built to service growth, even though such facilities may primarily benefit new residents. Developers who help create the new service demands are expected to bear some of the burden of the service costs they create. But many developers pass much of their development costs along to the new owners or occupants of their new developments. If developers should pay, how should they pay? Should each developer be required to negotiate with local governments (exactions) on each proposed development on a case-by-case basis, or should all developments be subject to a universally applied impact-fee formula? There are generational considerations as well. Should one generation have to bear the total service and facility costs for another? Should today's residents pay the entire costs of a facility whose benefits will extend beyond their lifetimes?

All of these policy considerations are inherent in the growth-financing decision-making process. They are also important in determining the appropriate mix of revenue sources needed to address growth's challenges, whether these sources be intergovernmental aid, local taxes, debt financing, or developer contributions. Given the complexity of the policy issues and the costs of most improvements needed because of growth, there is rarely one revenue source that can magically pay for the entire cost of major capital improvements. Impact fees, for example, cannot pay for all public improvements necessitated by growth.

In addition, the attitude of the city policy makers toward growth will have a significant influence. How highly valued is growth in the community? Should it be subsidized for the benefit of the entire community? How concerned are community leaders about lack of growth? Are they concerned enough to oppose impact fees because such costs to developers might discourage growth and investment? Such concerns were strong enough in Spokane, Salt Lake City, and Pueblo that there was no serious discussion of such fees in these cities during the decade. There is more discussion of economic-development strategies and community attitudes toward growth financing in chapter 6.

Inadequate Traditional Sources

General Obligation and Revenue Bonds. There are several reasons for why communities issue general obligation or revenue bonds. As noted in chapter 3, debt financing in the form of bonds is often used because cities cannot accumulate sufficient funds to build major facilities out of current revenue, either because of the lack of political discipline or because they need the up-front financing quickly to address immediate infrastructure needs. Using debt financing also allows the community to address intergenerational issues by spreading capital costs over several generations of beneficiaries and taxpayers. A systematic debt policy, such as the one adopted in Tempe (see the Government Finance Research Center's 1989 *Debt Capacity Study*), allows the city to spread bond-redemption payments over a long period of time. The policy avoids sharp rate increases and also allows the city to take advantage of the inflationary impact of debt service by redeeming the bonds with "cheaper dollars" in future years (Leithe and Joseph, 1990).

A bond is an agreement between a borrower (the city) and a lender (an investor). The lender buys the bond to give the borrower money now, and the city borrowing the funds agrees to pay the lender a fixed amount (or interest rate) yearly for a specified period of time until the debt is repaid (Fisher, 1988). Bonds have traditionally been attractive to investors because the interest earned on the investment is exempt from federal taxes. This allows bonds sold by local governments to be sold at lower interest rates, thereby indirectly subsidizing the expenditures of local governments by lowering the costs of being in debt (Bland and Yu, 1989).

There are two major types of long-term debt used by cities to finance infrastructure: general obligation bonds and revenue bonds. These two types of long-term debt are distinguished by the nature of repayment pledge made by the city selling them. General obligation bonds (GO bonds) are backed by the "full faith and credit" of the city issuing the debt, while revenue bonds are to be paid by revenue generated by the projects they finance, such as a sewer system or toll road. The use of revenue bonds has increased, especially since the advent of the property tax revolt, because they generally do not require the voter approval that general obligation bonds do (Bland and Yu, 1989).

As changes in the economic market made it more difficult for private development interests to secure debt financing, cities increasingly began to use their ability to sell tax-exempt bonds to finance non-traditional private or public-private projects. Chief among these private projects were economic development efforts, as well as pollution-control facilities built by private firms, private hospitals, and construction of low-income rental housing (Fisher, 1988). This practice increased to the point that, by 1984, "64 percent of all long term state and local bonds issued in the year . . . were for private purposes" (Fisher, 1988:249–50).

Congress reacted to this extension of the use of tax-exempt bonds by severely limiting the types of projects eligible for tax-exempt debt financing. The 1986 Tax Reform Act lowered the percentage of a bond's proceeds that could benefit a private interest from 25 percent to 10 percent; "lowered each state's volume limit for private purpose debt; [and] revoked tax exempt status for certain types of private-activity bonds, namely those issued for pollution control facilities, parking facilities, sports and convention centers, and industrial parks if any of the foregoing involves participation by the private sector" (Bland and Chen, 1990:44).

Cities still wishing to pursue debt financing for these types of projects must now either issue taxable municipal bonds (which generate higher costs to the city) or push the entire cost of the capital project onto private developers and seek private debt financing.

A further limitation on the use of tax-exempt bonds involves a 1988 U.S. Supreme Court case, *South Carolina v. Baker*, in which the court found that there was no constitutional protection for municipal bonds from federal taxation. While this exemption is currently still protected by federal statute, the court's decision effectively leaves this source of city revenue generation subject to political or congressional decisions rather than prior judicial decisions that had upheld intergovernmental tax immunity.

In its search to reduce the federal deficit and to eliminate tax loopholes, Congress has undertaken tax reform efforts that have had serious effects on local governments' ability to finance infrastructure improvements. Obviously, the desirability of a tax loophole is in the eye of the beholder. What is viewed as a drain on the federal treasury by some members of Congress, for example, is viewed by local officials as a vital source of capital for local government public works financing. Exempting interest income from taxation has a net negative impact on federal treasury receipts, estimated to be $8 billion to $10 billion per year (Wright, 1988). However, it also encourages local debt financing by providing a major incentive to bond buyers. Such tax-reform limitations, if carried to the extreme of removing the tax-exempt status of municipal bonds, could have a major negative affect on municipal capital-improvement programs and on cities' ability to respond to growth.

Grants. Federal grants were a major source of funding for state and local capital projects. At one time they constituted over 40 percent of state and local government capital expenditures (Leithe and Joseph, 1990). These grants were particularly important during the 1960s and 1970s, when several categorical grant programs were made available to local governments with little or no local matching requirements. Since the cutback in federal assistance, which began in the late 1970s, cities and other local governmental entities have had to rely on local sources for an ever-increasing amount of their capital financing. Admittedly, there are still a few federal grant programs that benefit infrastructure projects (community development, transportation, economic development, etc.), but they are of only limited help in financing the wide range of infrastructure needs facing local governments today. Some federal and state grants have been transformed into revolving loan programs that offer below-market interest rates at extended payback periods. The loan program funded by the U.S. Environmental Protection Agency to finance wastewater treatment construction projects is a good example. Loans obviously are less attractive than grants, but they are preferable to a total reliance on debt financing. Given the size of the federal deficit, it is doubtful whether federal grants will ever again become the major sources of cities' infrastructure financing they were in the 1960s and 1970s.

Taxpayer Resistance. Currently, debt financing is used in some areas of the country to offset the decline in federal assistance. However, debt financing is not popular in many parts of the United States. The taxpayer revolt, which began in the 1970s, continues to foster opposition to any tax increases. Of the bond issues that were on the general election ballot in 1991, half were defeated (Lemov, 1992). This anti-tax attitude has led many city officials to find alternative financing mechanisms that technically do not incur debt and are not required to be approved by the voters. Some of these mechanisms, such as lease-purchasing and revenue bonds, are discussed elsewhere in this chapter.

Taken together, all of these changes have severely limited the revenue options available to cities. The loss of tax-exempt status for some types of projects increases the cost of debt financing, and in times of increasing fiscal shortfalls means that more capital projects will have to be funded through alternative methods. Taxpayer resistance forces municipal entities to look to non-property tax revenue sources and to adopt revenue-generating mechanisms that do not require a public vote. Several of these alternative funding mechanisms are discussed in this chapter, such as user fees, interlocal agreements, payment in lieu of taxes, special districts and authorities, and developer impact fees.

Special Assessment Districts. There are several varieties of districts that local governments can create to provide services to a specially defined area. Since in most cases special assessment district debt falls outside of the tax-limitation measures discussed earlier and often does not require a referendum vote to approve the issuance of debt, it provides an important tool for cities seeking capital improvements. These districts are known variously as special districts, special assessment districts, and benefit districts. Special districts are "providers of one or more public services financed and administered separately from other local governments" (Porter, 1987:9). Special districts are relatively independent of other local governments and typically have their own governing boards separate from the local governing body (Urban Land Institute, 1989). Assessment districts, on the other hand, are extensions of local governments created in order to levy a special tax within a designated area of their jurisdiction that will primarily benefit from the proposed improvement(s).

Assessment districts usually do not have a governing board separate from the local government. The assessment on the property owners within the special assessment district is used as security on a loan to finance revenue bonds to pay for improvements.

INNOVATIVE FINANCING METHODS

There is a variety of financing methods used by cities for infrastructure financing. Their utilization largely depends on the particular mix of economic, political, and legal variables within each city. In addition, several other important factors restrict or reinforce municipal revenue-raising options such as a city's rate of growth, type of political culture, growth strategy, state and/or local spending or revenue limits, age, and sophistication of its planning process. A number of revenue options will be discussed in this section.

Public-Private Partnerships

The success of public-private partnerships in the financing of infrastructure components is typically dependent on community attitudes or political culture support for such a close working relationship between the public and the private sector in the provision of public services. Where private-sector participation in the implementation of community goals is seen as legitimate and to be encouraged, partnerships generally succeed. Where community attitudes force more of a separation between what is public and what is private in the community, the success of such partnerships can be tenuous at best.

These partnerships have become more significant with the apparent collapse of the federal-city partnership that emerged during the New Deal era and seemed to die during the Reagan and Bush administrations. According to an official with the National League of Cities (cited in Shafroth, 1989), the federal-city partnership was dissolved through the reduction and elimination of municipal federal grant programs at the same time that the national government continued to mandate functions and programs on cities.

It appears that in many communities, including those in the Urban West, effective public-private partnerships frequently have played a key role in stimulating and maintaining high growth levels and in supporting local government in matching infrastructure improvements and expansion with growth.

According to Apogee Research (1987), public-private partnerships can be either passive or active in character: "Active participation includes direct private investment and administration of a basically public responsibility such as the Babylon, New York, solid waste processing plant in which a private firm contributed part of the initial capital and administers the leased facility under the city's overview" (p. 13).

There are several forms of passive participation. One of the more prominent is one in which "investors 'own' a specific public works facility through their purchase of certificates of participation or equipment trust certificates—financial instruments backed by physical assets. The infrastructure itself is held by a trustee as collateral, and the user makes lease payments which, in turn, are used to pay debt service" (Apogee Research, 1987:3).

Lease-purchase agreements, which are increasingly popular, allow communities to buy infrastructure components, property, or equipment on an installment basis. This is accomplished through a contract with a non-appropriations clause that does not bind future councils. At least theoretically, each year a council may opt out of the contract. Practically speaking, however, this is not a very likely outcome for any community that values its bond rating. There are advantages to this approach in that the entity does not technically incur debt and can therefore avoid some debt-service costs because of the unique requirements of the transaction. Moreover, an election to approve the agreements is not required.

Special Assessment Districts

California has provided an assessment district option for cities seeking to finance public improvements that provides flexibility as well as a way around the limits of Proposition 13. This option is referred to as the Mello-Roos district concept. Created under the Mello-Roos Community Facilities Act of 1982, these districts are designed to "finance the purchase, construction, expansion or rehabilitation of any real or other tangible property with an estimated useful life of five years or longer" (Taussig and Associates, 1990:2). These improvements can include schools, fire stations, police stations, parks, libraries, major arterial roads, freeways, and water and sewer facilities.

The Mello-Roos legislation provides for the creation of Community Facilities Districts (CFD), formed

> for the purpose of financing infrastructure and public facilities through the levy of a special tax. All properties subject to the special tax are located within the CFD. [The special tax is a] levy on property owners within the CFD which is required to satisfy the debt service on Mello-Roos bond sales, or to pay directly for the construction of public improvements. (Taussig and Associates, 1990:2–3)

A single Mello-Roos district may involve several bonds. One unusual feature of a Mello-Roos district involves the "Mello escalator," which is "a component of the tax spread which lowers initial tax rates and eliminates large tax increases in a multi-bond program by escalating special taxes on an annual basis at a reasonable rate" (p. 3).

Another unique feature of the Mello-Roos district is that the benefit criteria—which apply to most assessment districts and dictate that improvements provide a direct and special benefit to the property owners in the district—do not apply in a Mello-Roos district. As such, Mello-Roos districts can fund major arterial roads and government buildings, for example, two uses of general benefit to a wider community (Taussig and Associates, 1990).

User Fees

Yet another way for cities to bypass revenue limitations is to shift the cost of providing services from general operating revenue to the users of that service in the form of user fees. The adoption of user fees is not new to the financing of transportation infrastructure. Toll roads and bridges have been used throughout our nation's history. Recently, however, states and localities have sought to pass an increasing share of the actual cost of maintaining the transportation system onto the users of that system. Many states now use a highway-users fund to share revenue with cities and counties for roads and streets. These funds are often based on gasoline taxes, motor vehicle registration fees, and various com-

Figure 5.1
Gasoline Taxes in Selected Urban West States, 1950–1990

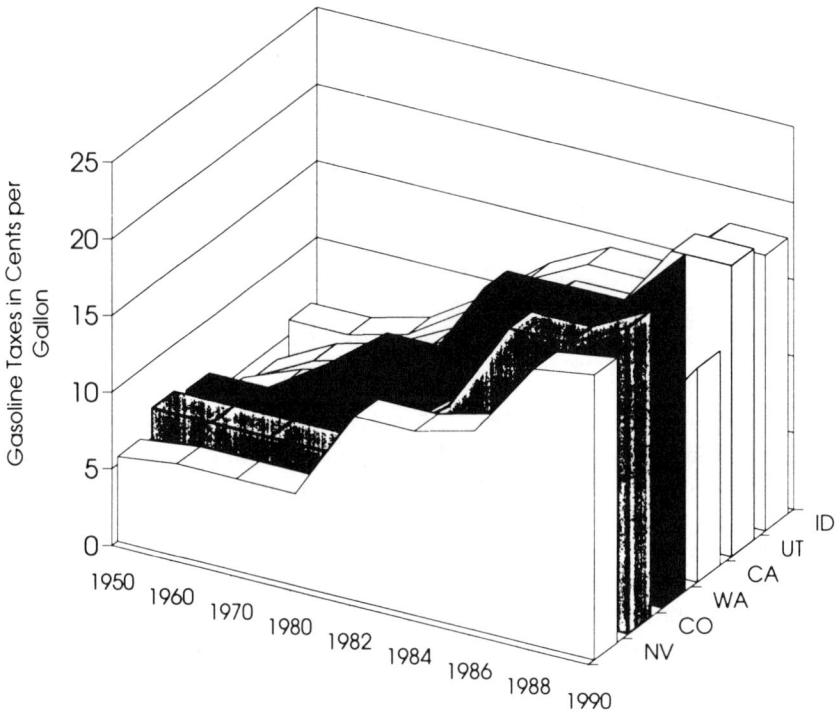

mercial motor carrier taxes and fees. The popularity of this form of revenue raising is evidenced by the fact that in 1989, eighteen states
increased their gasoline taxes. As user fees are often more palatable to
the tax-resistant public than increases in income or property taxes, states
have increasingly looked to hikes in highway-user taxes as a primary
means of funding roads and highways.

User Fees and Highway Funding

This source of funding for transportation has become very popular
with state governments throughout the nation, and all of the Urban West
states enacted a significant increase in their gasoline tax between 1982
and 1990. Figure 5.1 displays the rise in the state gasoline taxes in the
Urban West states in the years from 1976 to 1990. During the years 1984
to 1990, the most rapid increases in gasoline taxes took effect. As this
graph illustrates, states have increasingly looked to this user-based tax

Figure 5.2
Gas Tax Rates in Urban West Focus Cities, 1989

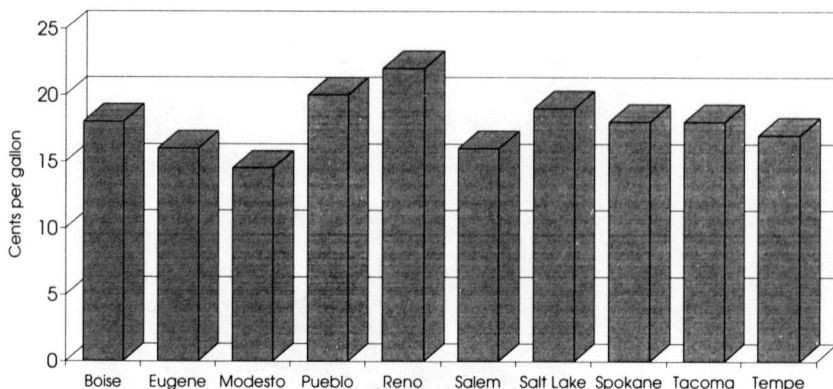

to fund their infrastructure. Figure 5.2 charts gasoline tax rates effective in 1989 in the Urban West states. The highest per-gallon tax on gasoline was in Nevada (22 cents), while the lowest per gallon tax was in California (14.5 cents). It is important to note that when the gasoline tax is determined by the state, cities may benefit through revenue sharing, but they have no determination in the rate of the gasoline tax themselves. In three of the cities examined in this study (Eugene, Salem, and Modesto), local option authority has been granted to add a local component to the gasoline tax.

Another source of highway-user revenue includes the fees and excise taxes assessed for the registration of motor vehicles. Figure 5.3 displays the deviation from the average motor vehicle registration fee for our ten focus cities. The average fee (for a new $10,000 car) was $159.41 in 1990. The lowest registration fees among the ten cities were found in the two Oregon cities and in Boise. In some cities, there was a local ad valorem component to the motor vehicle registration fee. The Attorney General's Office in Oregon, for example, determined that motor registration fees are charges imposed on property and therefore ought to be included within the new limits on property tax charges brought about by Measure 5. In Salt Lake City, the ultimate cost of registering a vehicle depends on what part of Salt Lake County a resident lives in and what the current levy rate is within that area.

Regional Approaches

Regional approaches to transportation issues are sometimes mandated by state actions that require county or regional coordination of transportation plans (see California's or Washington's new growth-manage-

Figure 5.3
Auto Registration and License Fees in Ten Urban West Focus Cities
(percentage of a ten-city average)

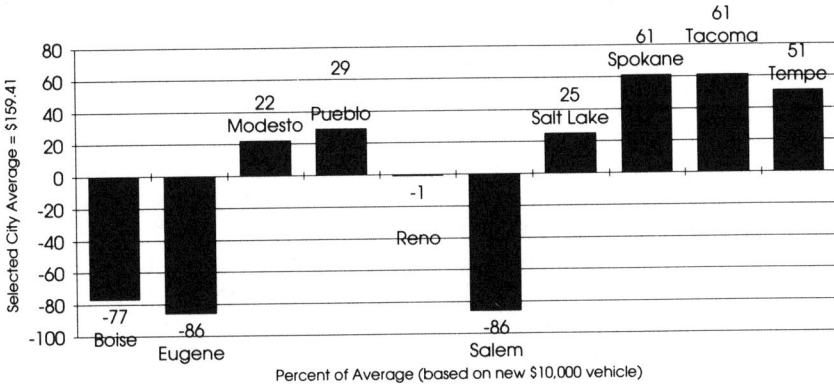

Percent of Average (based on new $10,000 vehicle)

ment law). Sometimes, state money is funneled to a regional body that either distributes that money to various localities or has direct street maintenance and development responsibilities. This is the case in Nevada and California. Depending on the nature of the state legislation or mandate, this may represent a further limitation of city powers. In some cases, however, a regional approach to transportation issues and funding arises out of a cooperative effort to provide funding. Interlocal agreements can ensure the sharing of revenue from one local government to another in exchange for the provision of some other service.

The City of Eugene and Lane County have worked out a revenue-sharing formula (the urban transition agreement) to allow the county to share its relatively healthy county road fund with the city. This is done in exchange for the provision of certain urban services by the city such as land-use permits in the urban transition zone or areas that are targeted for future urban development. The Lane County Council of Governments was key to the development of the urban transition agreement and provides staff support for the administration of the agreement and the development of the formula for sharing revenues. Eugene relied on this source of revenue for approximately 18 percent of its road and street budget in fiscal year 1988 (Oregon Department of Transportation [ODOT], 1990).

CASE STUDY: EUGENE, OREGON—USING INTERGOVERNMENTAL COOPERATION TO MEET COSTS

Among the innovations that cities have developed to meet the challenge of funding their transportation infrastructures are negotiated intergovernmental agreements. The staggering costs of repairing neglected streets and bridges, not to mention constructing new roads to meet the demands of growth, can often seem overwhelming. This case study highlights how one city and county have teamed up to share resources and expertise to the benefit of both governments.

The use of intergovernmental agreements to provide services has greatly expanded in recent decades. One study indicated that 52 percent of American cities and counties used some form of interlocal service contracts, which "involves the delivery of service by one unit of government for another on a payment basis." Joint service agreements, which are "agreements between two or more governments for the joint planning, financing, and delivery of services" were entered into by 55 percent; and 40 percent had been involved in service transfers, which "involve the permanent transfer of responsibility for a service" (Agranoff, 1989:141–42). This case study will highlight the use of one type of these agreements in Eugene, Oregon.

Eugene is a city of 112,669 approximately 110 miles south of Portland in the Willamette Valley. Eugene is actually part of a larger metropolitan area that includes its sister city of Springfield, located across the interstate. Home of the University of Oregon, Eugene has one of the highest percentages of college-educated residents in the country. Nearly 30 percent of those over 25 years of age in Eugene have completed four years of college, which is almost twice the national average of 16.3 percent (Eugene-Springfield Metropolitan Partnership, 1985). Historically, the area around Eugene has relied heavily on the timber industry, but recently it has begun to diversify its economy by attracting food processing and manufacturing industries (Eugene-Springfield Metropolitan Partnership).

The two cities of Eugene and Springfield have joined Lane County in a joint services agreement called the Urban Transition Agreement. Building on mechanisms put in place by the Oregon growth-management law, the Urban Transition Agreement calls for the two cities to provide certain urban services in areas of the county slated to become urbanized, while the county shares revenue obtained through state highway-user funds with those cities for their road funds (C. Anderson, personal communication, July 11, 1990). The Oregon land-use law requires each city and county to designate an urban growth boundary, which represents the outer limits for urban densities spreading outward from cities into unincorporated county land (see chapter 3). Both parties benefit from the Urban Transition Agreement. The cities get additional money for roads shared from the somewhat more robust county road funds, and the agreement ensures that city standards are met in permit processes and service provision in areas eventually to come into the city limits. The counties are relieved of the burden of providing extensive urban-level services in this area of the county, and they are ensured of the health of roads that are of regional importance for the area economy (*Urban Transition Agreement—Streets and Roads*, 1987).

While agreements of this nature are profitable to all in times of relative prosperity, the Urban Transition Agreement faces an uncertain future due to the recent property tax-limitation measure passed in Oregon. Whether Lane County will be able or willing to continue sharing revenue with Eugene and Springfield while facing the daunting Measure 5 property tax limitation of $10 per $1,000 of market value on each property remains to be seen. It is also likely that state-shared revenue with the counties will decline because one of the components of Measure 5 involves a shifting of the cost for public education from kindergarten to twelfth grade to the state, forcing substantial cutbacks in non-educational areas of state services.

Payments in Lieu of Taxes

Tax-exempt properties require general government services even though they do not contribute toward the cost of such services. In some cities the amount of tax-exempt property can be significant, raising important questions about who should bear the burden of paying for services to such properties. Salt Lake City officials struggled with this issue at length and commissioned a study to determine whether "the tax exempt status of the enterprise fund activities unfairly shifts the burden of public services from one group of residents/taxpayers to another" or, more specifically, from enterprise fund users to the property taxpayers. The consultant's report found that it did and recommended the creation of a system of payment in lieu of taxes (KPMG Peat Marwick, 1989). Based on this report and the work of the city's budget committee, the city council implemented a Payment in Lieu of Taxation (PILOT) system that imposes additional fees on the city's water, sewer, and refuse collection departments, which are then passed on to the users of these services as surcharges on their utility bills.

The intent of PILOT is to charge enterprise fund users a fee to partially reimburse the city's general fund for public safety and general governmental services. According to former Mayor DePaulis (1991:7), "[t]his charge will aid the City in reallocating the cost of providing services to tax-exempt entities such as churches, nonprofit organizations, and state and federal governments." Part of the justification for PILOT is the fact that all property owners, regardless of their tax status, pay for water and sewer services. The track record of this funding device in Salt Lake City over the next several years will be interesting to observe. There apparently is no comparable charge in any of the other Urban West focus cities. The importance of this payment in lieu of tax scheme must be kept in perspective. It is not a charge imposed on tax-exempt properties for all of the services they demand. Only the city's enterprise funds impose the charges, and it is done only for the purpose of reimbursing the city's general operating budget for services, such as billing, accounting, law enforcement, and similar support services provided to those enterprise funds.

Tax Increment Financing

Tax increment financing (TIF) is essentially a bootstrap approach to urban redevelopment and infrastructure improvement. It has effectively replaced the old federal urban renewal programs in many cities by providing revenue for public improvements in downtown areas. It is widely utilized in the West, especially among California cities. Its popularity has grown rapidly there since the enactment of Proposition 13, the California property tax-limitation measure passed in 1978.

TIF has become an integral part of the economic development and downtown revitalization strategies of many Western cities. Its popularity is partly based on the fact that despite the apparent association of tax increment financing with tax increases, it does not and cannot force an increase in taxes. A tax increment financing project pays for public improvements within a designated area that has been determined, through a public hearing process, to be blighted or economically underdeveloped. The public improvements made to such an area are financed through a rather complicated process.

When a TIF is created, the tax base is essentially frozen and all of the additional (incremental) revenue created by the expansion in the tax base due to public and private improvements in the TIF area are allocated to a dedicated fund to redeem the TIF bonds used to pay for the public improvements. TIFs fund a variety of public improvements, depending on the nature of the particular state enabling legislation. Typical TIF projects finance sewer and water extensions, land purchases, building demolitions, street improvements, and similar developmental activities. These improvements are financed through the issuance of tax increment financing bonds. The bonds are redeemed (paid for) through the incremental increase in revenue generated by the private investments and improvements in the area.

Tax increment financing involves a public-private partnership in which public improvements make private investments attractive, and private investments in turn produce revenue to repay the city for those public improvements. It entails a win-win situation for the city and the local business community in a wide range of settings. Paying for new streets, water and sewer lines, and other public services in a blighted area through TIF revenue can attract private investment that expands the district tax base and generates the revenue to repay the bonds. At times, such programs can displace homeless and low-income residents from blighted areas, and special attention is owed to this aspect of TIF projects in responsible cities.

There are a number of advantages to the TIF approach from the perspective of local government officials. Voter approval is not required. Tax rates are not increased. Redevelopment can be funded through local revenue rather than by relying on federal grants. There are some drawbacks, however. Since TIF projects are funded by diverting and not raising revenue, the district is wholly dependent on the tax rate decisions made by local governments whose levies overlap the area. The revenue coming to TIF areas can decline if the aggregate local government tax rates are decreased. Such decisions are not made by the redevelopment agency, but rather by locally elected officials from all of the local governments that levy property taxes in the area. The most serious challenge to district officials, however, is in estimating increases in assessed valuation. The TIF district's increase in assessed valuation has to be relatively rapid and substantial to generate sufficient incremental revenue to repay the bonds in a timely manner.

The growth of TIF has stirred some controversy. The number of TIF districts has grown so rapidly in California that county governments have complained about the adverse impact of these municipal programs on their revenue-raising ability (Simpson, 1991). The TIF mechanism is particularly irritating to county officials because TIF laws generally do not require a public vote and the creation of a district removes the potential for increased revenue to the area's local governments until the development bonds have been retired. As previously noted, the property tax revenue to local taxing districts are frozen during the life of the TIF district as an incentive to attract private investment. A county or school district, for example, would not get additional revenue from the increased tax base in the TIF areas until all of the TIF debt has been repaid or the authority for the TIF has expired.

Idaho's recently enacted tax increment-financing law helps address this issue by requiring the redevelopment agency to notify the taxing districts in the TIF area prior to the public meetings required for the creation of the district (Local Economic Development Act, 1988). Their input on the impact the district will have on other local governments is intended to generate support for improvements that will ultimately benefit all local governments. In Boise, TIF has played a key role in the city's redevelopment efforts. It was primarily through the implementation of a tax increment-financing scheme that the city was able to successfully implement its plan to redevelop the downtown core area. Revenue from the tax increment-financing plan paid the debt service for parking garages in the downtown area that were considered to be key for the completion of redevelopment efforts.

Developer Financing

Two types of developer financing mechanisms are widely used throughout the West: negotiated exactions and impact fees. Negotiated exactions will be discussed in this section, and impact fees will be analyzed in greater detail in the following section.

Negotiated exactions were among the first form of developer payments made to local governments. Such exactions go back at least to the 1920s, when local governments were authorized (or required) to engage in land-use planning and zoning (Nelson, 1988). As part of their planning process, local governments began to require developers to dedicate land or donate facilities or equipment as part of the permit approval process. The types and magnitude of exactions have proliferated since that time. In addition, the location of facilities supported by such payments has changed. Originally, exactions related to facilities, equipment, and land that benefited on-site facilities. Today, such payments are also required for off-site improvements that are affected by new development.

According to Apogee Research (1987:11), "[e]xactions have been expanded in recent years to include donations of specified facilities, construction of off-site infrastructure such as intersections and roads adjacent to the development, addition of low- or moderate-income housing units to the development project, and impact fees."

One of the real advantages of exactions to the city is that officials have almost complete flexibility. There are no guidelines for the negotiations process. Negotiations are done on a case-by-case basis and can result in a substantial contribution of private dollars for infrastructure. The downside to the developer community is that would-be developers are often placed in a near-blackmail situation. Typically, negotiations precede the granting of a building permit. Needless to say, developer bargaining positions are not strong at this point. It also means that without any mandated or approved set of guidelines, each developer can be treated differently. There is no predictability to the process. The requirements for one development do not necessarily set the precedent for another (Porter, 1986).

Impact Fees and Urban West Cities

There are numerous definitions of impact fees. They have been defined "as monetary payments made by builders or developers to jurisdictions in order to defray the public costs of providing infrastructure services to the development" (Nelson, 1988:ix).

Another definition is that they are "charges collected by a locality during its review of land projects to support infrastructure needed to serve
the proposed development" (Cervero, 1988:535).

Impact fees are, as their name implies, fees, as opposed to taxes. Such
charges are assessed on developers to pay for their proportionate share
of the costs associated with their developments vis-à-vis off-site public
improvements. Impact fees are one-time payments intended to be used
to pay part of the costs of wear on existing capital facilities or those
required to be built or expanded by such growth.

Cities and counties are increasingly turning to developer-paid impact
fees as an additional revenue source for their transportation budgets. The
National Council on Public Works Improvement (1988) counts impact
fees as one of the two best potential sources of increased funding for
roads.

Legal Principles

Some municipalities have pursued impact fee ordinances without specific state enabling legislation, but in testament to the constraints within
which cities must work, fee systems are most likely to be upheld in court
if enabling legislation exists and attention to the court-established conditions—commonly referred to as the rational-nexus test—have been
met. Legal challenges to impact fees have resulted in the following rational-nexus refinements as outlined in *Nollan v. California Coastal Commission* (cited in Nicholas, 1990:49).

1. A showing that new growth and development is expected over
   a time horizon (usually 5–20 years), and that new growth and
   development will require capacity expansion of the relevant capital facility;

2. Evidence that the fee imposed does not exceed a proportionate
   share of the cost the local government will incur to provide the
   necessary capital facility expansion to accommodate new growth
   and development; and

3. An assurance that the fee payer will receive sufficient benefit
   from the fees paid, in the form of the capital facility improvements that are built and which the developer will use within a
   reasonable period of time.

In other words, the rational-nexus test requires that there be a nexus
or relationship between the amount of the fee and the demand created
by the new resident or development. The rational aspect of this principle
requires that there be a finding that a demand is actually created and

that the resident or development will benefit from the facilities either improved or created as a result of the imposition of the fee.

The authority of cities to impose such fees is based either on state enabling legislation or municipal home rule powers (Nelson, 1988). Of the approximately half-dozen states that have enacted impact-fee legislation, five are in the West—Arizona, California, Nevada, Oregon, and Washington. Most of the major cities in California utilize these fees, as do many in Oregon and Washington. Nevada recently enacted into law such enabling legislation, and the City of Reno has imposed fees based on legislative guidelines (see the Reno case study). Recently, impact-fee legislation was enacted for the City of Boise and other local governments in Ada County, Idaho.

According to a survey conducted by the Government Finance Officers Association (GFOA), "the most popular use of impact fees is for sewer and water facilities, followed by parks and road" (Leithe and Montavon, 1990:x). The dollar amount of the fees charged ranges widely. Impact fees are only a portion of a package of revenue sources that support cities' capital budgets. According to the GFOA survey, the percentage of a city capital budget that affects fees varies from 42 percent in California to 5 percent in Texas (Leithe and Montavon, 1990).

Impact fees are not limited to road and transportation systems. In fact, cities in Florida, in conjunction with their concurrency doctrine (i.e., pay as you grow), have instituted impact fees for all major urban services. Under the concurrency doctrine, no new permits are to be issued unless fiscal capacity exists to fund all urban services at adopted levels of service (Bernhardt, 1990).

Unlike negotiated exactions, impact fees are the product of careful analysis of the proportionate costs of development. They are based on formulas that are applied uniformly to each type of development, residential, commercial, or industrial. These schedules are based on the assumption that they reflect the development's proportionate cost to local government. In fact, however, some scholars have argued that "due to legal restrictions or policy considerations, the fees recover less than the proportionate share" (Leithe and Montavon, 1990:3). Within these classifications, each type of development is charged the same fees. And with the exception of those schedules that are adjusted for inflation, the developers will generally have a good idea about how much they will be charged.

Most impact-fee systems either allow for or require the participation of an advisory committee that is involved early on in the process of formulating an impact-fee program. Another important feature of impact-fee systems is an accounting process that requires the dedication of impact-fee revenue for infrastructure affected by growth. Such systems generally set up a maximum time limit in which the impact fee funds can be spent. According to the GFOA survey, that limit averages 6.5 years (Leithe and Montavon, 1990). If the money is not expended within the designated time period, the impact fees are refunded to the developers.

Opponents of impact fees are often concerned that the fees place the burden of paying for capital improvements that all citizens will benefit from on newcomers alone (Porter, 1986). Others are concerned that developers will pass the costs of impact fees on to new homeowners or businesses, effectively pricing moderate-income homeowners and small-business owners out of the market. For example, an official from the Building Industry Association in Modesto related that his organization estimates that every $1,000 increase in the price of a home cuts out 100,000 buyers of that home state-wide (Paul Stewart, personal communication, June 1990).

It should be noted, however, that while some studies indicate that impact fees do add to housing costs (Singell and Lillydahl, 1990), others contend that the cost of developer fees are not passed on to home owners but rather have the effect of depressing the value of unimproved land (International City Management Association, 1988). This issue can be generalized to the tension between seeking industrial and commercial newcomers to a city (i.e., new development) while at the same time putting a system of fees in place that may scare off the development to a municipality without such fees. Other concerns related to impact fees center on the tracing of the paid fee to the provision of the capital project, which may be up to twenty years distant (Porter, 1986). To address this concern, many jurisdictions establish benefit districts to ensure that the money paid in fees is spent on projects of immediate benefit to the area of the new development (Nicholas, 1990).

Impact Fees in Reno

The City of Reno has recently adopted a system of transportation impact fees. The consultant's report on impact fees (Nicholas, 1990) utilizes a systematic methodology to meet the requirements of the court-developed rational-nexus test for impact fees. The city sought enabling legislation for the authority to use impact fees and was granted it in the 1990 legislative session (see the Reno case study below).

Impact Fees in Modesto

The City of Modesto's impact fees have been in place since 1988. In 1989 the city revised its impact-fee schedule, significantly increasing some of the fees. "Capital facility fees," as impact fees are known in Modesto, are utilized for several urban services, including police and fire, in addition to transportation (Modesto City Resolution No. 89–1132, 1989). Stanislaus County, where Modesto is the county seat, also recently adopted a set of impact fees.

Impact Fees in Salem and Eugene

Oregon's Land Use and Conservation Legislation, originally adopted in 1973, authorized the use of impact fees. The development of the land-use goals that are central to this legislation, however, delayed the implementation of impact fees until 1983. Measure 5 includes Oregon's impact fees in the revenue limited under the cap $10 per $1,000 of assessed value. Future implementation and revenue derived from this source, then, may change radically. The two Oregon cities involved in our study have had somewhat different experiences with the implementation of their impact-fee systems. While Eugene reports systematic implementation of its impact fees, with little organized opposition from the development community, Salem has a history of waiving or reducing its impact fees to ensure that development occurs (Wacker, 1990). Legislation passed in 1989 in Oregon restructured the way impact fees are calculated and assessed in that state, so current fees were unlikely to remain in place even before the passage of Measure 5. The 1989 legislation provided for reimbursement fees or fees for costs associated with capital improvements already constructed or under construction, as well as improvement fees, or fees for costs associated with capital costs to be constructed (League of Oregon Cities, 1990). Each of these fees, as well as their combination, are referred to as system development charges (Oregon House Bill 3224, 1989). The reimbursement fee is unlike any of the fees used in the other cities in our study, because it assesses a cost to newcomers for systems already constructed in addition to traditional means, such as the property tax assessment.

Impact Fees in Washington and Idaho

The state of Washington's new growth-management legislation passed in the spring of 1990 allows for the assessment of impact fees in several counties forcibly included in the growth-management plan (Washington House Bill 2929, 1990). In Idaho, the Ada County Highway District, which is responsible for the maintenance of Boise streets, has adopted a system of impact fees to help pay for the cost of transportation improvements. This was accomplished following the district's consideration of a consultant's report and public hearings (Duncan and Associates, 1990). The fee system was implemented in May 1992.

CASE STUDY: RENO, NEVADA—RAPID GROWTH AND LIMITED LOCAL DISCRETION

Local discretionary authority is virtually unknown among Nevada cities; Nevada's second largest city, Reno, is no exception. City charters are written not by local voters but by Nevada legislators. State law tightly controls most municipal functions, including finance. Under the conditions imposed by the 1981 tax-shift legislation, city property tax rates were reduced and state sales tax allocations to cities were increased. This shift has left cities heavily dependent on state aid. In 1991, state sales tax money constituted over 36 percent of Reno's total municipal revenue (Reno City Budget, fiscal year 1991). According to former Reno City Manager Hal Schilling (personal communication, 1990), "Reno stands alone among growth areas in not having local control." A recent national survey seems to back up Schilling's statement, if we include Boise, Idaho. Idaho and Nevada cities are close to the bottom in discretionary authority for the Urban West and for cities throughout the country (U.S. Advisory Commission on Intergovernmental Relations, see Table 2.1). This lack of local control puts such cities at a significant disadvantage in coping with the service impact of growth and maintaining a healthy fiscal condition. Reno has been largely unsuccessful in coping with and maintaining a sound financial condition. During the decade of the 1980s, Reno was unable to maintain a balanced budget. Surplus or one-time-only money was used to balance the budget (Nevada Legislative Auditor, 1986).

This northwestern Nevada city of over 130,000 is a council-manager government in Washoe County, not far from Sacramento. Reno has grown even though there is a significant strain of slow-growth or anti-growth sentiment in its local politics. According to recent census data, the city grew from 73,000 in 1970 to 134,000 in 1990, over an 80 percent increase. In the last three mayoral elections, the slow-growth candidate for mayor has won despite opponents who were heavily financed by developers. The current mayor's ability to make the elections a referendum on growth has succeeded "in a city already suffering from increasing traffic congestion and air pollution" (S. Voyles, personal communication, August 21, 1991). It is also important to understand the broader statewide context in which the growth debates have taken place. In recent years, Nevada has been the nation's fastest-growing state. Slow-growth in Reno does not necessarily have the same impact as in Modesto and other growth-conscious cities. While slow-growth advocates have served in the mayor's office and on the City Council, Reno has still increased its population by over 30 percent during this past decade. Reno's slow-growth mayor pointed with pride to his efforts to keep annual growth under 3 percent per year. Slow growth concerns in Reno center on limiting casino expansion to the downtown area and taking measures to improve the city's polluted air and congested streets (Sferrazza, 1991).

The imposition of a metered system for Reno's water is another issue tied to growth. Most of the water used in this city is not on a metered system. Opposition to the metered system takes many forms, but one of the most prominent arguments against the system is that water conservation will mean more water capacity for those who promote growth. Some hardliners would prefer to leave the water taps running than conserving water for the developers.

Payment for growth has been a major concern in Reno for the last several years. The implementation of a growth impact-fee system in Reno is a study in city-developer community cooperation. In close partnership, city officials and developers were able to gain legislative authorization in 1989 (Nevada Assembly Bill 372). Home-builder association support and a narrowly drawn piece of legislation modeled after laws in Texas were key to the adoption of the legislation (B. Thomas, personal communication, June 1990). Since the bill's passage, city officials, general contractors, home builders associations, and others have worked on a growth-impact system for Reno for the past several years. City planners and traffic engineers closely studied the city's major intersections to determine current and future traffic needs. City consultants analyzed alternative revenue sources and fee schedules to charge developers the proportionate share of their development's impact on the city's street system. Using the forecasting model MUNITRIPS, researchers were able to project over a ten-year period new growth and development in the city. They also analyzed the costs of improving the city's transportation system, projected revenue shortfalls, and examined the need for alternative revenue sources, with particular emphasis on impact fees. The data base for MUNITRIPS was the population and land-use projections developed by the city's planning department. The proportionate share of developer costs and a fee schedule for residential and non-residential land uses were compiled based on the population and land-use assumptions (Nicholas, 1990).

Before the system can be implemented, however, city officials are required to bring their existing road system up to their current level of service standard before charging new developments. The point of this requirement is that impact fees should not be used to correct existing deficiencies. This concurrency requirement, which is utilized in Florida and some other states, required the city to pass a major bond issue before it could impose an impact-fee system (S. Voyles, personal communication, August 21, 1990).

CONCLUSION

In this chapter we described some of the innovative and alternative methods of paying for infrastructure that cities have developed. Faced with continued demands for services and declining abilities to tax, cities have had to find new ways to finance their growth-impacted services. They have struggled to determine who should pay for growth and the most appropriate and effective financing methods. Included among the methods we discussed were impact fees and developer exactions, special assessment districts that allow the assumption of debt without a vote of the population at large, increased use of user fees, and regional approaches based on intergovernmental cooperation. We have also explored the rich variation in revenue mixes for transportation funding, from heavy reliance on the property tax in Salem and Boise to almost none in Tempe and Modesto. Highway-user funds are significant sources of transportation revenue in most cities, ranging from 54 percent in Tempe to 13 percent in Salem. Local option taxes are significant revenue sources for other municipal services in many of these cities, but not for the support of transportation infrastructure.

In chapter 6 we will explore economic development strategies among the Urban West cities and the responses made by neighborhood groups and others to what some citizens perceive to be a threat to their quality of life. Also included in this chapter will be a discussion of the political reform and political structure in Urban West cities.

6

The Role of Politics, Coalitions, and the Private Sector

After examining the many difficulties inherent in paying for growth covered in the last two chapters, it may seem odd to some readers that growth was nearly universally pursued by cities during the Urban West decade. Nevertheless, it is true that nearly every city of any size actively pursued growth, usually under the heading of economic development. We will discuss in this chapter some of the reasons that economic development strategies are so attractive to city officials, and how they go about seeking to encourage growth. Examples of approaches to economic development are highlighted in our case studies in Pueblo, Spokane, and Tacoma. All three cities battled to improve their image as business centers with aggressive economic development strategies.

The impact and costs of growth, as nearly every one of our case studies illustrates, often generate controversy. As growth accelerates, people begin to worry about a change in the quality of life in their community. For cities in the West, this community opposition to growth often represents a challenge to what had previously been an unchallenged partnership between business interests and city officials. This pro-growth partnership was made possible in part by the structures and institutions Western cities have inherited from the municipal reform movement active at the turn of the century. The challenge to the pro-growth coalition often comes from organized neighborhood groups. The role and impact of these groups on growth are explored in our Urban West focus cities.

PUBLIC-PRIVATE PARTNERSHIPS FOR ECONOMIC DEVELOPMENT

Economic Development Defined

As this section will describe, economic development is nearly universally subscribed to, yet seldom defined. As a policy issue, economic development appears to top the public agenda of most cities in the Urban West. During the late 1970s and 1980s, a consensus evolved among city officials about the need to implement economic development policies and strategies (Beaumont and Hovey, 1985). Communities arrived at this same consensus in a variety of ways (Fosler, 1988). Cities such as Pueblo did so out of desperation because of economic emergencies that required the development of aggressive economic development programs (Foster, 1989). The level of desperation to revitalize their economies was high enough in Idaho a few years ago that twenty-seven Idaho cities vigorously competed to have the state's new maximum-security prison located in their community. Not all cities pursue economic development out of desperation, but generally, cities feel they cannot ignore the economic development competition and need to broaden their tax bases and maintain their economic vitality (Judd and Kantor, 1992). It is conventional wisdom among local officials that communities either grow or die. There is no middle ground. The officials probably have not read *City Limits* but they seem to have instinctively adopted its economic determinism theme.

Economic development in some communities has become an end in itself. It has taken on almost sacred dimensions. A state municipal league director at one time wrote about the god "Eco Devo." Whether it has or will ever be worshipped in quite that way, economic development has been an important plank in the platform of most successful politicians. It appears that in the Urban West the question during many state and local campaigns has been which candidate could do a more effective job of promoting economic development, and not whether economic development should be one of the community's top goals (Bowman and Kearney, 1993).

Economic development is championed in many communities without a clear understanding as to what it means. Such ambiguity may also explain its widespread popularity in some communities. According to Bowman (1987:3),

"economic development" is a phrase that is widely embraced but seldom clearly defined. Conceptually, economic development has meant wealth creation to some observer, while to others, the phrase has signified material progress. As a goal, economic development ranges in meaning from tax base improvement to the redistribution of economic benefits to disadvantaged areas.

Beaumont and Hovey (1985:328) point out that economic development policies develop "without an underlying economic theory except that more jobs are good and less jobs are bad." More jobs mean more income generation and, presumably, more revenue for the city coffers. To the extent that economic development is perceived as promoting jobs and tax-base expansion, it is widely supported (Elkin, 1992). This interest in improving the community's employment picture is substantiated by a 1987 National League of Cities' survey; the mayors who responded believed that increasing jobs was one of their city's top priorities. The other major economic development goals included: tax-base expansion, job and business retention, and "achieving balanced quality growth" (Bowman, 1987:vi).

Economic development efforts can affect a community's social well-being as well as its economic health. Although only a small minority of mayors saw economic development as a way to redistribute some of the benefits to the poorer sections of their cities, equity and social well-being are goals in some cities (Bowman, 1987:vi). Elkin (1992:41) notes that in general, however, "one version of how to make a city grow dominates and others—which might either spread the costs differently or involve something other than rearranging land use with an eye particularly to downtown development—are given little or no consideration." Rather than helping to alleviate inequality, Elkin contends that the growth strategies themselves help to perpetuate inequality.

The degree to which cities lean toward economic or social well-being in economic development strategies is largely determined by the economic condition of the community. For example, mayors who place a high value on quality growth (that is, are willing to be selective about the type of growth pursued) are typically mayors of "cities that have stable, secure economies and that can afford to qualify the growth objective" (Bowman, 1987:11). There appear to be few examples of this in the Urban West.

Each community ultimately has to answer for itself what economic development means, what kinds of economic development strategies are appropriate, and what kinds of impact economic growth will have on it. After the community has made this kind of assessment, it can provide answers to the questions that will help determine the kind of economic development strategy that is employed: Will it be primarily the search for the relocation of businesses and industries from other areas, the creation of new businesses from within the community, or the expansion of existing businesses? These approaches are discussed further in the following section on economic development strategies.

Economic Development Strategies

The economic development strategies employed by cities focus on the following in varying degrees of emphasis: attracting new businesses and industries from other areas; maintaining existing businesses and encouraging their expansion; and creating new jobs and businesses from within the community (Beaumont and Hovey, 1985; Bowman and Kearney, 1993).

In trying to attract new businesses, cities attempt to develop a favorable business climate. They do not want to be viewed as hostile to business and precluding the opportunities for further growth. They want to project an attitude that is genuinely reflective of the entire community that growth is welcome and that businesses will not be frustrated by city development and regulatory policies in their efforts to grow.

City marketing strategies, aimed at attracting new business to the area, are often coordinated with state economic development efforts. Given the relationship of the cities to the state, state law provides the framework for whatever economic development policy a city adopts. Cities, however, can be far more specific in targeting their efforts than can the state. This is especially true in the kind of incentive packages a city might offer to a new business. Typically, tax relief can only be provided if state law allows the city such an incentive. Property tax breaks, for example, are ordinarily set forth in state law; so are other incentives such as tax increment financing or industrial revenue bonds. These mechanisms are not established by cities but by state law. State enterprise zones, in which areas are set aside with special tax breaks to encourage new business investment, are another example of state initiative incentives used at the local level.

There are a variety of incentive packages offered by communities in their efforts to attract new business. Typical incentive packages can include: technical assistance for the new business; relief from either state or local charges or taxes; customized job-training programs to prepare community people to work in the new businesses; public works participation through the extension of streets, water and sewer lines, and so on to new businesses; and a one-stop shopping approach in which new businesses can go to one office to get all of the information they need to develop or locate within a community. Urban West cities in general make wide use of these incentives.

Another economic development strategy involves the maintenance of existing businesses and the creation of new jobs from within the community. This approach to economic development is gaining greater attention among many local governments. In the past, many have focused almost solely on one aspect of economic development-relocation:

> As one economic developer noted, "We found that businesses were going out the back door faster than we could bring them in the front door." Most local areas are now concerned with business retention as well as attraction. And a growing number are asking: how can we facilitate new business starts and the expansion of businesses we already have? (Fosler, 1988:8)

An example of this technique can be found in Spokane, where the economic development group Momentum (described in the Spokane case study in this chapter) has sought to improve networking among area businesses to increase the use of local suppliers by local businesses. The result will be the retention of business opportunity and jobs.

Economic Development Organizations

Economic development organizations take on a variety of structural and organizational arrangements. The relationship between the private and public sector varies considerably, as does the prevailing view in the community as to the legitimate role of government in marketing the community and concluding economic development deals.

In some cities, the economic development function has been formalized into a municipal office or department. Economic development activities are an integral part of the city's budget. During part of our decade, the City of Boise allocated approximately $90,000 for an office of economic development (Mulady, 1990). In Salt Lake City, a city office of Local Business Advocacy "encourage[s] the retention and expansion of existing businesses ... [and] helps reduce bureaucratic red tape for businesses, and also facilitates the needs of special events and conventions" (Office of the Mayor and the Bear West Consulting Team, 1991:Appendix, 3).

Though some communities have organized their economic development programs around a single city office, partnership is a key element in most economic development arrangements. A city department or operation may be the only public-sector side of a public-private partnership. In Boise the private sector is represented by the Boise Area Economic Development Council, which plays a major economic development role in that city. Spokane's Momentum organization is an excellent example of how active and important the private sector can be in economic development efforts. (See the Spokane case study: Spokane—Gaining Momentum Toward Growth.)

Many other configurations are utilized. Some involve a mix of several types of public and private organizations: independent public agencies, private non-profit, and private for-profit organizations (Kane and Sand, 1988).

The challenge of these organizations is to develop a spirit of cooperation—a sense of unity, a common purpose, and a positive self-image. Projecting their image underscores the importance of public-private partnerships. Government is seen as playing a key supporting role. According to a Colorado economic development corporation executive (cited in E. Smith, 1989:20), government's role is seen as making an area "responsive to business needs. You're creating a product. Government isn't necessarily the best salesman; but it has responsibility for the tax structure, the economic environment, and providing educational and training resources."

Pueblo Economic Development Council's (PEDCO) Harvey Paneitz (cited in E. Smith, 1989:20) said that his organization needs "government support, because that's impressive" to the businesses they are courting. The point is that public-sector involvement makes clearer the image of a community whose attitudes are not anti-business.

In Salt Lake City, community leaders identified the fragmentation of their economic development effort as being a serious problem. In the first Salt Lake City Tomorrow exercise in 1987, one of the most important initiatives recommended was to foster a partnership that

> could provide a means for developing an overall policy direction to guide the future development of the Valley, and coordinating economic development roles between the range of government, private-sector, and non-profit organizations that now affect the Valley's economic development. (Center for Economic Competitiveness, 1987:3)

The problem they were concerned about dealt "with cases where conflicting policies of different agencies or government may create disincentives for growth, and could help to reduce duplication of efforts" (Center for Economic Competitiveness, 1987:3). Later that year, the Utah Economic Development Corporation, now known as the Economic Development Corporation of Utah (EDC), was founded with sixteen public and sixteen private memberships, including Salt Lake City (Office of the Mayor and the Bear West Consulting Team, 1991).

According to former Salt Lake City Mayor DePaulis in his 1989 state-of-the-city address, "the corporation is designed to bring meaning to the words 'economic development' and to act upon that definition in an organized, unified manner for all of Salt Lake County." It appears that the corporation is working quite well, even though some of the members, like Salt Lake City, are somewhat concerned about how many direct benefits they are getting (N. Pace, personal communication, 1991).

The kind of discord Salt Lake County has struggled with is not unique. Tempe and the communities in greater Phoenix have had similar problems. According to an article prepared by the Morrison Institute for Public Policy at Arizona State University (1990:51), the number of economic development organizations in the area contributes to a situation in which "competition and the lack of coordination still result in confusion among prospective businesses, and both the local and state economies have suffered the effects of lost ventures." According to Ken Western (1988:SE–1) of *The Arizona Republic*, a local business leader believed that "Arizona's 'smorgasbord' of organizations and commissions are ineffective, offer too many voices and operate on budgets that pale in comparison to those that operate elsewhere."

In its *Vision Tempe* effort, Tempe has sought ways "to further increase coordination and cooperation among these groups (thirty to forty organizations in the Valley) to make Tempe a more attractive place for potential and existing businesses" (Morrison Institute for Public Policy, 1990: 51).

Pueblo's unity in economic development effort stands out in marked contrast to the proliferation experienced in many Urban West cities. Pueblo has a public-private partnership that has worked, in large part, because of its successful attempt to speak with one voice in regard to Pueblo and the opportunities there. See the Pueblo case study, which details the city's success and the phenomenal efforts of its economic development organization, PEDCO.

CASE STUDY: PUEBLO, COLORADO—THE MAKING OF AN ECONOMIC DEVELOPMENT MACHINE

Pueblo, the "ugly duckling of the high plains," does not fit Colorado's idyllic mountain paradise image. Also known as Pewtown, this southern Colorado city, just south of Colorado Springs, is home to CF&I Steel Mill, once the largest mill in the West. Pueblo's Thirteenth Street is well known throughout the state as the entrance to the state mental hospital, which at one time had 10,000 patients. Colorado's strongest union town, Pueblo was once heavily influenced by eastern labor bosses and had noticeable Mafia activity (Peirce and Hagstrom, 1984).

This community is an important and interesting Urban West case study because of its successful fight to repair its image problem and its emergence as a major economic development competitor.

Pueblo is of significance not because it has faced the challenges of rapid growth but because it has survived the real threat of decline. Even though this southeastern Colorado city's population of 100,000 is about what it was in 1960, the real story is that it has not lost population. Pueblo's lifeline was cut a few years ago, but the community survives. Managing decline, or better yet, averting it, is the special challenge that Pueblo has faced during the past decade. The downsizing of Pueblo's major industry, CF&I Steel, and major layoffs at the U.S. Army Depot in the early 1980s could have devastated this once-thriving city. For much of this century, Pueblo was the second-largest city and the southern capital of Colorado.

CF&I was the largest employer in Pueblo and the largest taxpayer in the state of Colorado. At its peak, the firm employed over 6,000 people. It dominated the city and the county and gave Pueblo the look of being a one-company town.

In the early 1980s, the makings of a depression hit Pueblo. In a few short months, 4,000 jobs were lost at the steel mill and still others were lost at the Army Depot. Unemployment rose to 23 percent. These were devastating blows, and to some communities they could have been fatal. But out of this crisis came, according to one observer, a "war mentality" and an "efficient, blood-thirsty team" called the Pueblo Economic Development Corporation (PEDCO) (M. Lowrey, personal communication, June 1990). PEDCO's mission was to find new primary jobs to save the community. PEDCO quickly became one of the most aggressive economic development organizations in the country. PEDCO *is* Pueblo to the economic world. In this organization is combined all of the major public- and private-sector players in the area. Behind them has been a citizenry willing to tax itself to provide the public improvements necessary to attract major new industries to Pueblo. Since 1986, one-half cent per dollar (approximately $2.8 million) of city sales tax revenue has been dedicated to such improvements. That amount represents more money than the state of Idaho has appropriated for economic development efforts in recent years.

Pueblo's experience may or may not be a model for other cities, but it does illustrate the value of a united effort on economic development. Prior to the creation of PEDCO and the "Great Emergency," there were two competing economic development agencies, each wanting to speak for Pueblo. The situation was so bad that even Governor Richard Lamm visited the city to urge the competitors to unite (M. Lowrey, personal communication, June 1990). Today there is no question as to who speaks for Pueblo. According to PEDCO board member Walt Bassett (1987), "egos can be a serious detriment to economic development. . . . What we have here are competitors who are willing to work together for the good of Pueblo" (cited in Reed, 1987:5).

PEDCO is aggressive, and it can afford to be. Often, economic development organizations are accused of giving away the store (Beaumont and Hovey, 1985). But in PEDCO's case in the early 1980s, there was "no store to give away" (M. Lowrey, personal communication, June 1990).

In this private-public partnership, private-sector leadership appears to dominate. According to one economic development expert, the city, county, and water board are "on call for economic development needs" (M. Lowrey, personal communication, June 1990). When packaging deals with prospective industries, PEDCO promises the public improvements and then later figures out with the public entities how improvements can be made (M. Lowrey).

The result is that PEDCO has attracted five Fortune 500 companies and stimulated enough other economic activity to virtually replace most of the lost jobs (Chandler and Mills, 1989). Pueblo is now known for economic development in Colorado. It has the most aggressive economic development organization in the state, and it is the only city of its size to open a branch office in Southern California. It can make presentations within hours of learning about a company that is looking to expand or relocate. This effort has raised the self-esteem of citizens. Former City Manager Fred Weisbrod (personal communication, June 1990) says, "We no longer need a passport to get into Denver." *Pueblo Chieftain* Editor Chuck Campbell (personal communication, June 1990) says that "now Puebloans don't apologize about their town; they are proud." According to City Manager Lew Quigley (cited in Reed, 1990:52), "Economic development has changed the attitude of this community. . . . No matter what the crisis, everybody knows in Pueblo that we don't have to be second rate to anybody."

Economic Development and Federalism

According to Bowman (1987), our federal system, which features division and separation of powers, encourages the kind of competition we are seeing today among the communities. Federalism provides the context in which economic development is undertaken: "The interaction of federalism and capitalism structures economic development" (p. 7). The American capitalist system, with the free flow of capital across artificial boundaries, encourages pursuit and competition among communities for economic development. Bowman (1987:3) goes on to say:

Cities are porous. . . . They are affected by the actions of other governments—national, state, and local. The economic development-related activities of these other governments structure city government's behavior. For example, when the national government reduces Urban Development Action Grant funding or a state government creates enterprise zones, the effect is felt at the local level. City governments have to design their economic development strategies within the "rules of the game" established by other levels of government.

Local economic development strategies have to take the actions of the national government into account, as many federal programs have a local impact. In the National League of Cities (NLC) survey, 60 percent of the mayors indicated that governmental intervention "had a major or significant effect on local economic health" (Bowman, 1987:63). The impact of the national government can be either positive or negative. Federal grants can play a significant role in helping a city put together an attractive offer (Bowman and Kearney, 1993). Projects are often funded out of several federal grant sources.

Leveraging is an important practice in urban economic development. It means that city officials have been able to use federal funds as a lever to raise additional funds from the private sector to help support development activities.

However, national government policies can have a major negative effect on cities. According to Bowman (1987:23), the Reagan administration's "massive disinvestment from America's cities and towns" has resulted in a loss of substantial portions of municipal federal funding. Some key municipal programs that have supported economic development efforts have been severely reduced or eliminated. The Community Development Block Grant (CDBG) program is an example of a federal aid program that has assisted many cities throughout the country in helping to revitalize their downtown areas, improve their housing stock, and construct public facilities. The Urban Development Action Grant (UDAG) program was eliminated by the Reagan administration although the program provided an important leveraging capacity for cities to combine their resources with that of the private sector. Bowman (1987:24) states that

> from its inception in 1977 through 1986, the leverage ratio for UDAG was estimated to be $6; that is, for every $1 of public funds invested in UDAG projects, another $6 in private money was generated. Over the long haul, these projects translate into employment opportunities, a revitalized cityscape, and increased tax revenues.

Federal funding has positive effects both literally and symbolically. The allocation of federal dollars had the effect "of getting the local economy moving. CDBG funding and UDAGs tend to promote confidence in a community as a place for investment. They have come to symbolize the federal government's commitment to America's cities and towns. Their diminution suggests the reverse" (Bowman, 1987:24).

Cuts in the Economic Development Administration, the restriction on certain industrial revenue bonds, and the termination of the General Revenue Sharing program seems to have had a negative influence on cities. According to the NLC survey, almost 90 percent of the respondents agreed that their economic development programs will suffer as a result of these cuts (Bowman, 1987).

Effectiveness of Economic Development Efforts

The long-term effectiveness of economic development campaigns and organizations is the subject of considerable controversy. It is hard to dispute the effectiveness of the PEDCO effort in turning the city's economy around. After losing 17,000 jobs during a fifteen-year period, with an unemployment rate at 19 percent in 1982, according to a PEDCO official, "[w]e had our backs against the wall" (Foster, 1989:1). To accomplish a major turnaround, the community has undertaken an extraordinary effort. Former PEDCO Chairman Harold Mabie cited three major reasons for Pueblo's revitalization: (1) free land, which was offered to companies that would locate at the spacious Pueblo industrial park; (2) employee training, which the president of Pueblo Community College offered to customize for any new firm with the support of state grants; and (3) "one-stop shopping," by which PEDCO streamlined the permit-granting process. PEDCO officials point with pride to the experience of two Target warehouses. One warehouse was located in Pueblo and was in operation before the other in California could get all of its permits (Foster, 1989).

The final chapter on Pueblo may not be so rosy, however. The community has been turned around, but at what price? Will the short-term gains be converted into long-term successes? Will this mean long-term economic advantage or will it mean only a temporary respite from a continuing decline? Could some of the resources have been better spent on such things as the community's infrastructure and other public facilities and services? What will be the long-term effect of the so-called giveaway programs?

Some say that aggressive economic programs and incentives are misplaced and that their approach is fundamentally flawed (Rubin and Zorn, 1985). Paul Peterson (1981) notes the widespread support for economic development policies, although he asserts that much of what affects these cities—that is, the welfare of the larger economy and the ultimate movements of labor and capital—is beyond their control. Scholars have noted that cities tenaciously pursue economic development activities, especially tax-reducing inducements to attract business, although studies have shown that tax incentives are not a major factor in business location decisions (see Smith et al., 1992, for a review of these studies; also see Swanstrom, 1989). Smith et al. (1992:540) contend that state and local politicians are "loathe to criticize the argument that tax incentives are beneficial, or to question the effectiveness of the other instruments which attempt to promote economic development for fear that the first to say 'no' will be excluded from whatever growth does take place in the national economy."

How critical are some of these incentives to the decision-making process? Are they high on the list of considerations of companies looking to relocate? Or are they unnecessary add-ons that have no real impact, except to drain the community of resources that could be more wisely and efficiently utilized elsewhere? Judd and Kantor (1992:489) note that one result of economic development strategies is that

> public poverty increasingly exists side by side with private plenty. Corporate towers, waterfront recreational development, enclosed shopping malls, luxury hotels, stadiums, and new convention centers have sprung up in cities all across America—while cities struggle to balance budgets, maintain infrastructure, and provide services.

One needs to be cautious about making generalizations about the success of these organizations and, in many cases, it may be too early to be able to know. A judgment made about an economic development program may need the benefit of several years' experience before its true effectiveness can be measured.

> Measuring success in economic development is not easy. There is confusion as to just what success is. For example, some cities point with pride at a revitalized central business district and claim successful economic development. Other cities count up the number of new firms and declare victory in the economic development wars. Others talk about renewed community spirit as a sign that economic development has been successful. One way out of this measurement quagmire is to link success to the achievement of goals. (Bowman, 1987:57)

Looking at the Urban West focus cities, it becomes clear that there are some things these cities have done in the way of economic development activity that would be helpful to them whether or not they relocated any new businesses in the community. For example, the strategic planning process that many of them have gone through has given them a good understanding of their strengths and weaknesses as a community. (See the Salt Lake City case study, which focuses on the long-range planning that has taken place in that community.) Of our focus cities, Boise, Spokane, and Tempe have undertaken planning processes that have been beneficial to their economic strategies.

It is interesting to observe some communities improve their self-image and confidence in dealing with the outside world through their economic development strategies. Boise, Tacoma, and Pueblo are good examples of this. All of them, not too long ago, were cities whose residents seemed to apologize for them. In 1974 Boise was featured in an article in *Harper's Magazine* as a city that had destroyed itself through misguided urban renewal policies (Davis, 1974). The characterization probably was not fair, but given public sentiment around that time it may have been fairly accurate. Today, most Boiseans point with pride to the number of high rankings they have received in national magazines. Pueblo is another example of a city that has transformed itself from the "ugly duckling" of the plains to a major economic development competitor and a city of people who no longer believe that they "need a passport to get into Denver" (F. Weisbrod, personal communication, June 1990).

For a look at Tacoma's attempt to shed its negative image see our case study on Tacoma, Washington. Whether the improvements to the city's image justify the expenses and forgone revenue of their economic development programs remains an open question.

CASE STUDY: TACOMA, WASHINGTON—IN SEARCH OF LIFE BEYOND THE "TACOMA AROMA"

For some cities, rapid population growth presents an opportunity to create a new, improved city image and economy. This case study describes the changes and challenges facing the city of Tacoma, Washington, where civic and community leaders hope to use their recent growth spurt to fuel comprehensive aesthetic and economic improvements to their downtown and waterfront areas. Tacoma's situation highlights the uncertainties that surround growth and economic development. Many cities have hoped for the renaissance that Tacoma is planning. However, as noted earlier, cities can persuade and entice, but jobs, investments, and tax revenue are dependent on the whims of private decision makers (P. E. Peterson, 1981). Whether Tacoma's blend of federal, state, local, and private money and construction will lead to the economic and cultural revitalization the city hopes for depends in large part on economic forces and decisions out of its control.

Tacoma is a city of 176,664 (1990 population) on the shores of Puget Sound and within sight of Mount Rainier, which is in the same county. The region has historic ties to the forest products and agriculture industries, but recently shipping, high technology, and recreation have been cited as important emerging industries (Tacoma–Pierce County Chamber of Commerce, 1988). The Port of Tacoma has grown to become the sixth-

largest container port in North America and the twentieth largest in the
world. The port estimates that 19,000 jobs in Pierce County are related
to its activity (Port of Tacoma, 1989). Recently, the Port of Tacoma lured
away the Port of Seattle's largest tenants, Sea-Land and Evergreen Lines,
bringing Tacoma nearly even with Seattle as a container port (P. O'Malley, personal communication, August 6, 1990).

Only thirty-six miles south of Seattle, Tacoma has lived much of its
existence in the shadow of its larger and more prosperous neighbor.
Tacoma's image has often been the butt of jokes from other Washing-
tonians, who ridiculed the "Tacoma aroma" emanating from the industries on the waterfront and the downtown's lack of appeal. The *Seattle
Weekly* reports that as far back as the 1930s, when Tacoma tried to beau-
tify its downtown by installing street lights, it was dubbed "the best-lit
graveyard on the West Coast" (Moody, 1991:41). Even fans of the city
are critical, such as Fred Haley (a "lifelong Tacoman"), who says of his
city, "It's got nowhere to go but up" (cited in Moody, 1991:41).

This persistent negative image has not, however, stopped Tacoma
from being swept up in the skyrocketing growth of the Puget Sound
region. As chapter 2 noted, Tacoma was one of the nation's four fastest-
growing cities in the last decade. The Puget Sound's growth has been so
rapid that the Washington State Legislature passed a growth-management law in 1989 that forced counties and cities surrounding the Puget
Sound to plan together, address housing and transportation shortages,
and force new growth to pay its own way through impact fees (Washington State Growth Management Act, 1989).

Population is not the only sign of growth in Tacoma. Along with the
port success noted earlier, the city has successfully attracted $458.3 mil-
lion of local, state, federal, and private investment in its downtown revitalization plan (Moody, 1991). Less tangible but also important is the
growth of what City Manager Ray Corpus called a "can do attitude"
(personal communication, July 25, 1990). This has led to what Moody
refers to as a heightened sense of consensus about what Tacoma's downtown ought to be. Plans include a remodeling of the city's Union Station
Railroad depot, a theater district, a University of Washington branch
campus, a state museum, and an expansive and unusual pedestrian
walkway that will connect the downtown to the waterfront by passing
over freeways and industrial areas.

The guarantee, "if you build it they will come," doesn't, unfortunately,
apply to downtown revitalizations. Tacoma has attempted major projects
to draw business and conferences before, as in its 1981–1984 building
spurt, which included a downtown Sheraton and a financial center. The
lure was in place, but "no one showed up" (Moody, 1991:48). After ten
years, these projects are barely breaking even. Paul Peterson (1981)
points out that cities, unlike nation states, have no way to control several

processes critical for their survival: the movement of people in and out of their boundaries, and the movement of capital in and out of their boundaries. Tacoma is hoping that its substantial public investment will be the catalyst to private-sector jobs and investment. But businesses will react to larger economic changes. As Moody remarks, "The city's fate, after all, rests less on the visions and tastes of its citizens than on regional and national forces beyond its control" (p. 49).

REFORM GROUPS AND THE URBAN WEST

The second major topic in this chapter is the emergence of neighborhood-based reform groups in the Urban West cities. As the introductory paragraph to the chapter pointed out, many of these groups have organized around opposition to development projects and growth. The result is that in some cities the officially sponsored economic development efforts are opposed by neighborhood groups within the community. To understand the development of these neighborhood groups, it is necessary to look at the structure of government typical of most Western cities and how dissatisfaction with that structure has led to increased neighborhood political activity. As the next section describes, many Western cities have government structures first made popular in the progressive reform movement.

The Progressive Reform Era and the Urban West

The urban reform movement that took place around the turn of this century, often referred to as the Progressive Reform Movement, left its impact on the structure of city government in the West. Western cities are essentially products of these early reform efforts, even though some of them were not even in existence when the movement was at its peak.[1] The major components of the reform platform discussed in this chapter include council-manager forms of government, non-partisan elections, at-large elections, and civil service reform.

The turn-of-the-century reforms were directed at the excesses of the big city machines found in the East and Midwest. Patronage, corruption, and inefficiency were among the concerns of these primarily middle-class reformers.[2] To address these problems, the reformers supported proposals to place more emphasis on the interests of the entire city, not just particular sections or wards. They were also concerned about corruption related to partisan politics in city government, the patronage system that supported party dominance, and the inefficiency in government that resulted.

At bottom, these middle-class, business-oriented reformers wanted government to operate like a business, free from partisan political bickering. To them, municipal government was more analogous to a private corporation than a political organization. They believed politics should be taken out of city government, and that this would lead to greater efficiency. There was no Democrat or Republican way to pave streets or extend sewer lines. These were technical matters, not political ones (Hill and Mladenka, 1992). According to the early reformer, A. D. White (1992: 205),

> the questions in a city are not political questions. They have reference to the laying out of streets; to the erection of buildings; to sanitary arrangements, sewerage, water supply, gas supply, electrical supply; to the control of franchises and the like; and to provisions for the public health and comfort in parks, boulevards, libraries, and museums.

Therefore, the argument went, cities should be led by professional city managers who would answer to the city council, which would be the policy-making body. Managers should not be political leaders but coalition builders. They should be skilled in administration. Echoing the argument of Woodrow Wilson (1887) for a separation of politics and administration, managers would not be policy initiators but implementers. They should be chief executive officers to their board of directors, the city council. According to Holli (1992:241) these reformers wanted to

> change the structure of municipal government, to eliminate petty crime and vice, and to introduce the business system of the contemporary corporation into municipal government. Charter tinkering, elaborate audit procedures, and the drive to impose business efficiency upon city government were the stock-in-trade of this type of urban executive.

Efficiency was also sought through changes in the way city employees were hired. A merit-based employment system replaced the traditional patronage method of hiring city workers. This system would allow employees to be judged on their abilities and intelligence, rather than political affiliation and contributions.

The reformers also proposed significant changes in municipal electoral systems. In the spirit of removing politics from city government, they advocated non-partisan city elections. In some cities, however, party organizations remain active in supporting candidates, and although officially non-partisan, party labels are known. An example is Pueblo, where one council member admitted that everyone knows who the Democrats and who the Republicans are, despite their non-partisan elections (S.

Corsentino, personal communication, July 27, 1990). The same might be said for Salt Lake City and Boise. Everyone knows that former Salt Lake City Mayor Palmer DePaulis is a Democrat; in fact, in the closing days of his administration, he announced his candidacy as a Democrat for governor. Non-partisan former Boise Mayor Dirk Kempthorne is now the Republican U.S. senator from Idaho.

The Progressive reformers also favored at-large electoral systems, whereby candidates are elected in city-wide contests. A. D. White (1992: 206) wrote,

> I would elect the common council by a majority of all the votes of all the citizens; . . . instead of electing its members from the wards as at present—so that wards [that are] largely controlled by thieves and robbers . . . can control the city. I would elect the board of aldermen on a general ticket, just as the mayor is elected now, thus requiring candidates for the board to have a city reputation.

In addition, Hays (1992:63) wrote that the "ward form of representation was universally condemned on the grounds that it gave too much influence to the separate units and not enough attention to the larger problems of the city."

These elements of reform were effectively backed by the National Municipal League, created in 1894, which provided assistance to reform groups and established a model city charter that helped provide the impetus for adoption (Welch and Bledsoe, 1988).

Adoption of reform elements spread across the country but were more "widely adopted in the West and Middle West, where machines were less well-entrenched and the reforms simply seemed a way to make government more efficient" (Welch and Bledsoe, 1988:8). In reviewing the most recent survey data from the *Municipal Yearbook* (DeSantis, 1990), one finds that Western cities are more likely to have reform structures than cities from other regions. Of the cities in the population range from 100,000 to 200,000 (the size of the Urban West cities), the clear majority are reform cities.

Council-manager systems, popularized in the Progressive Reform Movement, are very prevalent. Only Boise, Salt Lake City, and San Bernadino of the thirty-four Urban West cities are not council-manager cities. The electoral systems of Urban West cities also reflect the impact of the Progressive Reforms. Of the thirty-four Urban West cities, twenty-nine conduct non-partisan elections with candidates either being elected at-large or with a combination of at-large and district elections. A number of cities have adopted mixed electoral systems. According to MacManus (1985:484),

mixed systems are attractive to reformers who are unwilling to go
so far to endorse exclusively single-member districts, which they
regard as merely "wards in sheep's clothing." At the same time,
they are increasingly reticent to defend exclusively at-large councils
when they appear to have the effect of diluting minority representation.

For example, in Pueblo there is a mix of district and at-large elections.
Half the council is elected at-large and the other half by district election.

Reform and the Pro-Growth Coalition

Getting the politics out of city government and diffusing the power of
ward-based politicians through reforms, such as by non-partisan at-large
elections, made way for a new set of interests to gain power in communities. As noted before, cities in the West are more likely to have
reformed institutions and electoral systems. Ross, Levine, and Stedman
(1991:152) note that in many cities, particularly in the Sunbelt, "[o]ne
notable consequence [of reform] was the access that reform institutions
afforded booster or growth coalitions." These coalitions were composed
of business owners, chambers of commerce, the local media, and city
officials. Spokane, Washington, provides a good example of a reform city
with a very strong coalition of business and city officials seeking pro-
growth options. The case study from Spokane, which follows this section,
illustrates the connection between the business community and city officials in that city.

Reformed city government institutions that avoided politics made the
link between city governments and growth coalitions almost inevitable.

Nonpartisan government, whether the weak mayor-council form,
the commission system, or city-manager government is usually
somnambulistic government. For, it is a form of government that
fosters a quiescent, acquiescent citizenry, where only the business
community and the property-owning middle class need be politi-
cized. (Lupsha and Siembieda, 1977:185–86)

Indeed, non-partisan elections, especially those held separate from the
traditional election schedule, have very low voter turnout, giving extra
influence to the special interests with a stake in the outcome of the election (Ross, Levine, and Stedman, 1991). The special interests with a stake
are often the business and real estate community supportive of pro-
growth policies. Elkin (1992:45) describes the impact that the connection
between growth-oriented development interests and city officials has on

who has power within communities. He contends that in the area of land-use issues there has been a

> failure of popular control [and] the battlefield of city politics is not flat but is tilted toward an alliance of public officials and land interests. Those who would want it any other way must push uphill, whereas such an alliance only has to sit still and wait until the task of pushing the rock up the incline grows too burdensome.

This alliance is described by Molotch (1976) as a growth machine that rarely succumbs to citizen activism (see also Fainstein and Fainstein, 1983; and Mollenkopf, 1983 for a similar argument). Nevertheless, groups have arisen in some cities to contest the power of the growth machine. This is discussed in the section after the Spokane case study.

CASE STUDY: SPOKANE, WASHINGTON—GAINING "MOMENTUM" TOWARD GROWTH

Spokane is in eastern Washington, only several miles from the Idaho border. Its population has grown slowly from 170,516 in 1970 to 177,196 in 1990. Its growth rate for that period was 1.04 percent, that is, nearly no change. Spokane maintains its historic ties to the agricultural and timber industries in eastern Washington and northern Idaho, but has since developed thriving industries in health care and higher education (B. Gray, personal communication, June 20, 1990). The city first leapt into national and regional prominence when it was host to the 1974 World's Fair. This event required major redevelopment of a large section of its downtown, turning former railroad switching yards into the still-popular Riverfront park (Gray). According to Jack Geraghty, a former Spokane County commissioner and now director of the Citizen's League of Spokane, the World's Fair was made possible largely because of the financial commitments made to the project by the "old money" families that owned the major corporations and newspapers in Spokane (personal communication, June 21, 1990). The prosperity and growth attached to the World's Fair soon fell off, however, and the city entered a long period of stagnant growth, being especially hurt by the recession of the early 1980s. In response to this situation, business leaders in Spokane turned to the method that had worked so well for the World's Fair thirteen years before: putting the private sector to work for the city. The result was a group called Momentum.

Momentum is the result of a group process entered into by 110 business and community leaders in Spokane in 1987. After hiring a nationally recognized group facilitator, these leaders locked themselves in a conference hotel for a weekend to address how to get Spokane's economy moving. This group process featured a consensus-type decision-making process in which 75 percent of the participants had to agree before any one strategy was adopted (S. E. Meyer, personal communication, June 20, 1990). The result was a set of ten primary strategies oriented toward two simple goals: creating more jobs and increasing income for area residents (Momentum, 1989). The top three strategies for reaching those goals were diversification of the Spokane economy, increasing tourism, and increasing capital availability (Meyer, 1990).

Momentum works by collecting money from area businesses committed to improving the economy, and channeling that money to existing agencies that implement the strategies, such as the Spokane Area Economic Development Council and the Convention and Visitors Bureau (S. E. Meyer, personal communication, June 20, 1990). A letter accompanying Momentum's 1989 annual report indicated that in the three years since its creation, Momentum collected and invested $2.5 million of private money toward economic development in the Spokane region (Clack, Cowles, Redmond, and Zirkle, personal communication, 1989).

How successful has Momentum been in stimulating the Spokane economy? In the three years since Momentum began its five-year plan, 8,900 new jobs have been created in Spokane, several big-ticket businesses such as Boeing and Seafirst Bank have located operations there, small businesses have moved to Spokane, and the gap between Spokane's median income and the nation's has narrowed (Clack et al., personal communication, 1989). Momentum's largest success, however, may be in creating and solidifying the positive outlook on jobs and growth for Spokane that now seems pervasive among Spokane's leaders. Momentum's 1989 annual report explains the joint efforts and public-private cooperation that made this unique effort effective: "The success of Momentum belongs to all of us, . . . to the volunteers who created the plan, . . . to the agencies who put the plan into motion, . . . and to the investors who believed in the plan and made it possible with their money."

Reactions Against the Growth Coalition

Growth has come under attack in cities where some residents have not appreciated or perceived that there were benefits to growth. With the concern about the direction of city policies has come the attempt to reform the "reform" institutions of cities. Cities like Tacoma and several others in the Urban West have enacted "reforms" such as district elections designed to break the link between growth coalitions and city hall. The at-large elections supported by the earlier reformers are now being questioned for their bias toward the wealthier candidates who can afford to run a city-wide campaign (Ross, Levine, and Stedman, 1991). In other cities, "the power of the city manager's office has come under attack" (p. 153).

In addition to attempts to change the structure of city government, neighborhood organizations are emerging as significant forces challenging the growth coalition in a number of cities in the Urban West. They are often fueled by citizens' perception that local officials are no longer responsive to their needs. Recall that GOAL, the citizen group described in the Modesto case study, was formed in part because of the perception that the city council was unduly influenced by the development community (P. Mensinger, personal communication, July 19, 1990). Growth-related issues are often the reason that neighborhood groups organize (Logan and Rabrenovic, 1990), although the focus of their concerns and activities vary widely from city to city.

Regardless of what part of the country they are in, neighborhood organizations are often created in response to a crisis or perceived threat to the quality of life in the neighborhood. According to Logan and Rabrenovic's (1990) review of neighborhood associations, proposed land-use changes seem to be the primary motivating factor that stimulates the creation of organizations—a specific

industrial/commercial development, [a] residential development [or a] transportation problem [that] typically involved disputes over the rezoning of land to a higher density or from residential to non-residential use. [The transportation issues] referred to "intrusions" into the neighborhood environment, rather than availability of transportation services. (p. 77)

These are clearly the sorts of changes often associated with growth and economic development projects. Opposition to these kinds of developments may be the reason neighborhood groups are counted among the actors in city economic development politics described as troublemakers by Bowman (1987).

Neighborhood groups, once organized, often make use of initiatives and recalls to achieve their goals electorally. In doing so, they make use of direct democracy devices put in place by the progressive reform movement, which made the pro-growth alliance they oppose possible. Ross, Levine, and Stedman (1991:153) describe this irony when they write:

The structural reforms of non-partisan, at-large, managerial government enhanced the power of progrowth forces in the Sunbelt. Yet another set of reforms—the initiative, referendum, and recall—provided the possibility of direct popular action that eventually brought an end to the period of unchallenged booster dominance in many Sunbelt cities.

In some of the urban politics literature, the assumption is made that the natural antagonists of the neighborhood organizations are the developers and others involved in proposing and making land-use changes. However, "(t)he relationship between neighborhood associations and land developers also may be complex," and conditions will sometimes bring developers and neighborhood groups into alliance with each other (Logan and Rabrenovic, 1990:71). There are references in some studies to developers and neighborhood associations having cooperated, particularly in instances of "gentrifying city neighborhoods" (Logan and Rabrenovic, 1990:71).

Neighborhood organizations are not always created out of opposition to city hall. In some cities, in fact, the city itself has encouraged or participated in their formation. Officially sanctioned neighborhood advisory groups have been used in several large cities, such as New York City and Washington, D.C. (Ross, Levine, and Stedman, 1991). Western examples of large cities that use official neighborhood organizations include Portland, Tucson, and Phoenix. Portland and Tucson have been among the leaders in establishing strong neighborhood organizations (Haeberle, 1989; Morrison Institute for Public Policy, 1990). Tucson established a neighborhood assistance office in 1969, and in 1990 had registered 135 neighborhood groups. The office had a staff of six and a budget in 1990 of $277,000. Phoenix recently created such an office with a $135,000 budget and three staff members (Morrison Institute for Public Policy, 1990). Cities use neighborhood groups as

> channels of communication, sources of legitimation, vehicles of social control, and a means to organize and direct resources. This need has grown as the ideology of emphasizing local participation and control has become more widespread. Of course, cooperation may tend toward co-option. (Logan and Rabrenovic, 1990:70)

The effectiveness of these organizations in opposing growth-related issues is somewhat controversial. Recall that Molotch (1976) claims that the growth machine rarely succumbs to citizen activism. Others note that neighborhood groups are sometimes able to "stall the growth machine" (Logan and Rabrenovic, 1990:69). It is certain that increasing numbers of cities have passed growth-limiting measures in recent years, many of which appear to be the result of citizen mobilization (see Donovan and Neiman, 1992; Glickfeld and Levine, 1992, for a review of recently passed growth measures).

The Urban West and Neighborhood Organizations

Neighborhood activity has been on the rise in the Urban West focus cities. The Modesto case study in chapter 3 provides an example of one group that successfully used the initiative process to slow growth in its community. Three of the ten focus city planning departments—Boise, Modesto, and Tempe—reported that their city had active neighborhood groups opposed to growth (see Table 3.1).

Tempe is another example of a city in which neighborhood organizations are becoming more prominent in city politics. In 1987 the city established a Neighborhood Assistance Program, and later it established a Neighborhood Assistance Office. The purpose of the office has been to encourage "associations to develop a neighborhood plan and block watch to fight crime, study zoning issues and foster neighborhood clean-up and beautification" (Tseffos, 1988:B–1). Existing neighborhood associations had been formed to fight a proposed commercial or housing project in the neighborhood. This observation reinforces Logan and Rabrenovic's (1990) assertion that groups are often formed around concern over a single land-use issue. City officials report that development issues are becoming more contentious in many neighborhoods, and there is greater resistance in many of the neighborhoods to any change that is perceived to negatively affect the quality of life (Garcia, 1987). Beyond these transitory issues, city officials were concerned that without greater neighborhood activity, the quality of some of the older neighborhoods would decline (Tseffos, 1988), an example of how city hall may attempt to use neighborhood groups to their mutual advantage.

Several neighborhood groups in Boise have been active in combating proposed developments in their area. Five neighborhood associations and a number of other civic groups have become important players in development-related issues. Over 100 volunteers associated with the East End Neighborhood Association became involved in a dispute over a proposal that appeared to threaten potential parkland (A. Peterson, 1992). Other issues that have given rise to citizen protest include proposed shopping centers close to residential areas and proposed development in environmentally sensitive areas, particularly wetland areas. Proposed development in the rolling foothills bordering Boise on the north and east has raised concerns in established neighborhoods that would experience major traffic increases.

Of the recent Boise foothills developments, two have particularly raised controversy—Hulls Gulch and Castle Rock. A proposed development in a previously undeveloped area called Hulls Gulch in the Boise foothills spawned a coalition of neighborhood and environmental groups that raised their political activity to a new level of sophistication: "They ran their efforts much like a political campaign. They printed signs, bumper stickers, and press releases, and relied upon ordinances and case law to support their position" (J. Fuhrman, 1990:24). In spite of their increased efforts, the subdivision was approved by the city. In this case and another proposed foothills development, the groups are now pursuing a new tactic of purchasing the threatened areas in trust (J. Fuhrman).

Though their influence is not always clear, the effects of neighborhood groups and citizen activists on public policy making in Boise may increase. The recent Boise Visions planning process may reflect prevailing community attitudes. The group recommended that "Boise city should encourage the involvement of neighborhoods in policy development, and explore the possibility of formalizing their role in the process" (Boise Visions Steering Committee, 1992:296).

Neighborhood groups may have also contributed to changes in attitudes of voters and city officials toward growth. The last election in Boise in 1991 resulted in the election of a "slow-growth" (as opposed to a "no-growth") candidate to the city council and a close race for an incumbent who was expected to win easily until his opponent made an issue of the contributions he had received from developers. The day after the election, *The Idaho Statesman* (1991:7) editorialized that the message of the election was that "Boise voters want a council that will weigh developers' proposals carefully and listen to citizens' concerns."

CASE STUDY: SALT LAKE CITY, UTAH—MANAGING GROWTH AND DECLINE

Salt Lake City remains the most populous city in Utah, even though its neighboring Salt Lake County cities have made significant population gains while Salt Lake City has lost almost 30,000 people over the last three decades. In 1960, Salt Lake had 189,000 people. In 1990, it had 159,936. Meanwhile, Salt Lake County grew from 458,607 to 725,956 from 1960 to 1990. In fact, Salt Lake County provides "urban services" to approximately 260,000—more people than does Salt Lake City (M. Stewart, personal communication, June 1990).

Despite these numbers, Salt Lake's place in Utah and in the intermountain West has not been diminished in several important respects: It is still the area's major transportation center, the capital city of Utah, headquarters of the Church of Jesus Christ of Latter-Day Saints, home to the University of Utah, and the center of commerce for the state. Even though the city has only a little over 20 percent of the county population, it employs almost half of the county residents. It generates almost 40 percent of the taxable sales in the county and 20 percent of the statewide total (Salt Lake City Department of Finance, 1989).

Salt Lake serves as an interesting case study of a central city that faces the problems of a stagnant tax base, "a fractionalized economic development effort, and outmigration" (Office of the Mayor and the Bear West Consulting Team, 1991:1). A review of recent Salt Lake City history illustrates the intractability of public policy problems. Jake Garn, who served as mayor in the early 1970s and resigned in 1974 to become a U.S. senator, dealt with many of the same types of issues the city is struggling with today. His administration was concerned with the problems of governmental fragmentation, and during his tenure the city struggled with the need to broaden its narrowing tax base (Alexander and Allen, 1984).

These issues were still major agenda items for the city's recent strategic planning process, which was conducted during the administration of former Mayor Palmer DePaulis during the late 1980s and early 1990s. DePaulis felt the city was at a crossroads. In his state-of-the-city address in 1989, DePaulis aptly summed up the real meaning of such a planning process for his community and perhaps for most communities throughout the country. He said:

[T]oo often in the past, we have let others write our story and define us. The definition has not always been flattering, nor has it always been accurate. My message tonight, therefore, focuses on the chapter *we* want to write for our community, on the definition we want to pen for ourselves. Because if we do not purposefully set out to write our own chapter, it will surely be written for us. It is the time to say to ourselves and to the world, *this* is who we are. This is what makes Salt Lake City unique among all other cities in this nation.

In this process of defining or redefining themselves, planning participants dealt with such major issues as "broadening the tax base through economic development efforts" (Office of the Mayor and the Bear West Consulting Team, 1991:17), developing stable and adequate revenue sources, and overcoming the conflicts and competition among so many different local government entities. Increased economic activity did not translate into major revenue increases, due to a state revenue-sharing formula that rewarded population increases as much as it did the volume of retail sales. In this equation, the central city, Salt Lake City, lost revenue to the rapidly growing bedroom communities surrounding it. State-mandated sales tax and property tax exemptions also reduced potential revenue. Finally, despite increased economic activity, property tax values were relatively stagnant. Proposals to deal with these problems included a change in the distribution of sales tax revenue to cities and expanding local government revenue-raising authority.

One of the real problems was the lack of interlocal cooperation in the county. Political leadership had become fragmented with the proliferation of so many local governmental entities and political leaders who had their own turf and agendas. Business and economic leadership was more oriented toward private-sector concerns and had not developed a unified voice on economic development in the region. No consensus existed over a regional economic growth policy and the role each entity should play (Center for Economic Competitiveness, 1987:1). Some of these concerns seem to have been addressed by the creation of the Economic Development Corporation of Utah, a unified economic development organization that appears to speak for both the public and private entities of the Wasatch Front. But some of the concerns of Salt Lake City officials have centered on whether these efforts directly benefit their city (N. Pace, personal communication, June 1991).

Economic development remains a major priority in the Salt Lake area and is supported as a way to solve the city's long-term fiscal problems and to ensure that Salt Lake City benefits from the revenue it generates by its own tax base. But a 1990 update of the Salt Lake Tomorrow project indicated a perceptible change in priorities. Economic development was still important, but the residents were more focused on "neighborhood 'liveability,' government efficiency and regional cooperation to resolve cross-jurisdictional problems" (Office of the Mayor and the Bear West Consulting Team, 1991:3). Residents were particularly concerned about major developments in the city and how they might change "the character of their neighborhoods" (p. 7). Improving intergovernmental cooperation, though a somewhat elusive goal, had support even to the extent of consolidating city and county governments, a proposal that had been placed on the ballot in several elections.

In his last state-of-the-city address, the retiring Mayor DePaulis (1991) took a somewhat philosophical view of his strategic planning efforts and what his city could accomplish in both the short and long term. He said:

[W]hether we are seeking the Olympic bid or managing our city, I liken us to the long-distance runner, rather than a sprinter. Our goal, unlike that of the sprinter, is not just a few yards ahead. It is miles before us. We have to pace ourselves and to keep focused on the goal over the distance. Two years ago, in my 1989 State of the City remarks to you, I said that our city had begun gathering economic momentum. It was a pleasure and a relief to finally be able to talk about growth, following the sobering budget we had faced as a result of federal government cutbacks and requirements. The momentum I referred to in early February of 1989 continued through that year and through 1990. We are building again. We are moving again. Construction cranes, those loveliest of mechanical birds, are perched throughout our downtown.

He concluded by saying, "With our mind's eye toward the future and a road map in our hands, we most certainly will create the enthusiasm and the energy to attain our goals."

CONCLUSION

In the introduction to this book, the literature on urban politics was described as having elements that perceived cities to be primarily products of economic determinism. That is, cities were described as seeking policies that would benefit their economic health and growth (Paul Peterson, 1981). We pointed out, however, that other scholars contend that there is an important and critical role for local political forces in city decision making (Wong, 1988). The themes we addressed in this final chapter illustrate the strength of both of these approaches to urban politics. Without a doubt, concern for economic development is nearly universal among city officials. Yet as we also saw in our discussion of neighborhood groups opposed to growth, sometimes local political forces do prevail.

That local officials continue to employ aggressive economic development strategies in spite of only modest evidence that they successfully attract new business lends support to the pervasiveness of the economic determinism theme. Economic development is not cheap for cities. They must not only pay the direct costs of the economic development office itself, but they must also forgo large sums of tax revenue used in tax breaks and incentives. If the economic development strategies work, and growth in jobs and population results, then the city must assume the costs of paying for the infrastructure necessary to support the growth. Chapters 4 and 5 outlined the difficulties in paying for infrastructure when the pace of growth outstrips the city's ability to pay for the infrastructure demanded by new population and businesses. Nevertheless, it is a rare community whose city officials decide to slow or stop their economic development activities.

Examples of cities willing to underwrite large costs to finance economic development activities are found in our case studies of Pueblo and Tacoma. Both have aggressive plans and strategies, and both have set aside substantial resources for their efforts. Whether either city has achieved economic development success, however, is difficult to determine. Evaluating success is made difficult by the lack of a concrete definition of what economic development is supposed to accomplish. This is perhaps illustrated by the frequently cited idea that an improved city image or heightened civic pride are evidence of the power and worth of economic development efforts. Certainly, some jobs and wealth are created through these development programs. The question of the effectiveness relative to the costs to the city, however, remains open. What opportunities are lost to Pueblo in dedicating one-half cent per dollar of local option sales tax revenue exclusively to economic development? What other things could have been done with that money? What if Tacoma rebuilds its downtown and the people and businesses do not come? These are the costs and risks of economic development.

There is a pervasive notion that what is good for the local business community economically will be good for the city. This may well be true, as healthy businesses mean an improved tax base and more tax-paying citizens. Increasingly, however, citizens in Western cities are questioning this perspective. The pro-growth alliance that thrives in the progressive reform-era structure of most Western city governments has been recently challenged by neighborhood groups wielding an alternative view of the mission of the city. The close partnership between city officials and business leaders, illustrated in the case study of Spokane, is in some cities being confronted by neighborhood groups concerned about the impact and cost of development. Competing visions of how much growth is good and what impact growth will have on quality of life pit neighborhood groups against development interests. City officials, previously nearly always on the side of the development community, now must seek a finer balance or risk running afoul of increasingly sophisticated initiatives and candidates fielded by active neighborhood groups. The importance of local politics in these issues is the root of the literature challenging the economic determinism theme in urban studies.

That cities are recognizing that they must adapt to these changes is demonstrated in the use of city hall–based neighborhood organizations. The combative nature of the relationship between city officials and neighborhood groups is reduced as the organizations become part of the city's policy-planning process. This use of neighborhood groups is illustrated in our case study of Salt Lake City, where neighborhood organizations are an integral part of strategic planning in the city.

Do economic forces predominate in the Urban West, as Paul Peterson suggests? Our study of the Urban West focus cities suggests that while economic factors are important and help explain the priority placed on economic development there, other non-economic issues are also of considerable significance. Tempe, Modesto, Boise, and Salt Lake City have active neighborhood organizations that help balance the scale between economic growth and quality of life. Even in Pueblo, which has strongly supported economic development, there continues to be a strain of dissent, yearning for more of a balance in the allocation of resources.

Cities are limited in their range of policy choices. They are often at the mercy of forces beyond their control, we suspect that they generally understand these limitations. But there is so much activity in the Urban West that one would not know how limited they are by the efforts that are being made to improve cities and the visions that are being created for the future.

NOTES

1. The Progressive Reform Movement is usually considered to have lasted from approximately 1890 through 1930 (Welch and Bledsoe, 1988).

2. For a review of the class bias of the Progressive Reform Movement, see Hays (1992). Other scholars have suggested that the Progressive Reform Movement was also rooted in white ethnic fear of the immigrant-controlled political machines. The reforms, most of which were designed to remove power from the machines, also had the effect of diminishing the power of the growing immigrant populations (see Judd, 1988).

7

Conclusion

The themes of this book are the limitations imposed on cities and their struggles to implement policies and maintain services during a period of rapid growth in the West. As discussed in the preceding pages, cities are largely bound by the constraints of federalism of either the state or national government, by the national or international economic system, and by initiatives of citizen activists.

Federal and state policies and actions have had a major impact on cities, much of it to limit the authority or discretion of city officials. Federal urban policies have had their limiting effects in a variety of ways. Federal mandates on cities, including air- and water-quality requirements and changes in municipal bonds procedures, rose during this period. The federal courts also imposed significant restrictions, particularly in limiting municipal bond authority and requiring municipal compliance with federal employment legislation (Fair Labor Standards Act). In addition, federal funding for a variety of city programs diminished or disappeared during our Urban West decade. New urban policies may emerge that will be more beneficial to cities than Reagan's New Federalism, but such policies will no doubt be limited by the federal government's need to get its own financial house in order by implementing even more tax increases or revenue enhancements that will preempt or considerably limit local revenue-raising ability. The implementation of national domestic policies will require city assistance, probably through more federal mandates that may or may not include reimbursements.

As far as state government limitations are concerned, Dillon's Rule is still alive and well in the Urban West in the latter part of the twentieth century. Even cities with home rule authority are still largely dependent on or limited by state law as far as basic city operations like revenue raising and annexation powers are concerned. In chapter 2, we noted that state laws and constitutional limitations, along with the initiative process, have brought property tax limitations to cities. In chapter 4 we discussed the decline in the quality of municipal infrastructures and the funding limitations and growth pressures that led cities to shortchange their spending on infrastructure, especially transportation infrastructure. Two case studies on Salem and Tempe helped illustrate challenges inherent in this policy arena.

As noted by Paul Peterson and others in the political economy urban literature, cities are driven by a powerful logic to compete for scarce economic development opportunities. Chapter 6 detailed the considerable resources and efforts devoted to this policy arena by our focus cities—Tacoma, Spokane, Pueblo, and Salt Lake City. The cities' economic context will require much attention to the necessity for survival and the need to compete for scarce economic resources. That does not mean, however, that cities are no longer viable governmental entities and that the policies developed by cities are not inherently interesting in and of themselves. Cities will continue to struggle, to grow, and in so doing will in many ways confirm the Paul Peterson hypothesis. The "unitary interests" (Paul Peterson, 1981) will continue to predominate and provide the key to understanding the policies and decision making in many communities.

However, with the growth we have discussed among the Urban West cities have come more complexity and diversity in local policy making. Conflict is becoming more of a significant pattern at the local level in an increasing number of communities. Citizen groups are questioning and in some cases effectively channeling growth-oriented leadership and their policies. The "growth machine" may not necessarily be the wave of the future for every city. Conflict may impede this heretofore irresistible force. Local initiatives, either on the ballot or in other forms, could play an even greater role in the setting of local policies. Tax policy, development, and land-use decisions may become more and more the province of the bumper sticker and electoral campaigns in popular elections than those of a closed elite in any given community.

City governments are also limited by the actions of their citizens. They know how to use and are using in increasing numbers the direct democratic devices fashioned by the reformers at the dawn of this century.

Chapter 2 detailed the impact of citizen initiatives during the property tax revolt on city fiscal decision making. Chapter 3 noted that only a handful of growth-management measures begin and end in the city council chambers. Most are imposed by state legislatures or by citizens taking direct action, all against a background of a changing economic environment. Our case study of Modesto illustrated how that city's citizens responded to rapid growth and imposed growth restrictions through the initiative process. This case study and other discussions pointed out how complex notions of local autonomy and democracy have become today. Local autonomy, which has been largely associated with granting more discretion to local officials, has taken on a greater dimension. Greater citizen activism at the local level means that citizens have taken more of a direct role in policy making, particularly as it relates to growth and the financing of that growth.

The Urban West in the Twenty-first Century

One of the real challenges facing cities will be to maintain or expand the fruits of some of the existing efforts. Will the current economic development policies result in permanent tax base increases and job creation, or will there be yet another round in the economic development wars? Will communities pitted against communities find that this war is more "zero-sum" than "win-win"? What will the long-term effects be of tax concessions and fee write-offs? How attractive will they appear to residents twenty years from now when the facilities built for important business prospects are left vacant by yet another restructuring or a company finding yet a more enticing offer? How beneficial will the current public-private initiatives look to citizen activists when it may appear that only short-term private economic interests were served by the investment of public resources in the way of tax expenditures and public official time spent in collaborating with chamber economic development campaigns? What will the bottom line be for public services and local treasuries when communities get a better perspective on the costs of growth?

With conflict and diversity comes the need for political leadership and brokering skills that in many cases only a local political entity can provide. The sphere of the political may not be large today but it is emerging, even as the world becomes even more interdependent and the pressures of national and international decision making become even more evident. The fledgling planning efforts undertaken in some of our Urban West cities may by necessity become an integral part of each community. A concern for the future dominated many of our discussions with cities and the publications they shared with us. Several of our focus cities had participated in or were considering "futures" commissions such as "Vision Tempe," "Boise Visions," and "Future Spokane." Others reported day-long retreats to better define the mission of the city and the objectives that would help the city reach its goals. There is a recognition of the need for forward-looking approaches, whether that be in regard to future growth patterns in land use, capital-improvement planning, future revenue sources, or working with neighborhoods for future planning and zoning needs. Not every city is able to break the short-term cycles of budget years and election cycles, yet most realize that only by anticipating the future will the city avoid falling prey to its limits.

With the renewed emphasis on planning has come the drive for more local discretion on financial decision making and the need to diversify local tax bases. Alternatives to the property tax for financing infrastructure were explained in chapter 5. The general movement in many cities away from sole reliance on the property tax has led them to adopt new ways to obtain funds needed for growth-affected public facilities. Some of the alternative financing techniques explored included user fees, impact fees, local gas taxes, and an intergovernmental cost-sharing arrangement highlighted in the case study of Eugene.

Another aspect that emerged from our study of how cities are coping with their limits is a movement toward cooperation instead of confrontation. Chapter 6 described how cities and the private sector have pooled their resources to seek economic health. We found cooperation, not only in formal agreements sharing powers or responsibilities, but in the development of informal arrangements and relationships among intergovernmental and private-sector actors. Our case study of Eugene described a formal agreement on sharing funds that benefits two governments working together. As noted in chapter 6, cooperation between the public and private sectors is critical to making economic development and privatization schemes work. Consistent themes we found about cooperation were: a recognition that problems are often regional and require the input and cooperation of all affected governments; an acceptance of the common goals of the private and public sectors in regard to economic development and willingness to work together; and a recognition of the need for cooperation between citizen groups and the city.

Bibliography

Agranoff, R. (1989). Managing intergovernmental processes. In J. L. Perry (ed.), *The Handbook of Public Administration*. San Francisco: Jossey-Bass, pp. 131–47.

Alexander, T. G., and Allen, J. B. (1984). *Mormons and Gentiles: A History of Salt Lake City*. Boulder, Colo.: Pruett Publishing.

Anderson, C., Director, Public Works, Eugene, Oregon. (1990, July 11). Personal interview.

Anton, T. J. (1989). *American Federalism and Public Policy: How the System Works*. Philadelphia: Temple University Press.

Apogee Research. (1987). *Financing Infrastructure: Innovations of the Local Level*. Washington, D.C.: National League of Cities.

Association of Washington Cities. (1990). *Comparison of State Growth Management Systems*. Paper presented at the Growth Strategies Conference, Renton, Washington, April.

Barber, P. (1992). A community without economic growth is one short on opportunity. *Idaho Statesman*, April 26, p. 1F.

Barker, M. (ed.). (1984). *Rebuilding America's Infrastructure: An Agenda for the 1980's*. Chapel Hill, N.C.: Duke University Press.

Battaille, K., Planner, Salem, Oregon. (1991, March 6). Personal interview.

Beaumont, E., and Hovey, H. A. (1985). State, local and federal economic development policies: New federal patterns, chaos, or what? *Public Administration Review*, 45, 327–32.

Bernhardt, R. C. (1990). The Florida concurrency doctrine: Blessing or boondoggle? *The Real Estate Finance Journal*, Spring, 51–55.

Bland, R. L., and Yu, C. (1989). Acquiring and repaying debt. In J. L. Perry (ed.), *Handbook of Public Administration*. San Francisco: Jossey-Bass, pp. 337–56.

Bland, R. L., and Chen, L. (1990). Taxable municipal bonds: State and local governments confront the tax-exempt limitation movement. *Public Administration Review, 50,* 42–48.

Boas, P. (1990). Firm raises bond rating for Tempe. *Tempe Daily News*, Jan. 21, p. B–1.

Boise City Finance Department. (1990). *Comprehensive Annual Financial Report*. Boise, Idaho: Boise City Finance Department.

Boise Visions Steering Committee. (1992). *Boise Visions Final Report*. Boise, Idaho: City of Boise.

Bollens, J. C., and Schmandt, H. J. (1975). *The Metropolis: Its People, Politics, and Economic Life*, 3rd ed. New York: Harper and Row.

Bowman, A. O'M. (1987). *The Visible Hand: Major Issues in City Economic Policy*. Washington, D.C.: National League of Cities.

Bowman, A. O'M., and Kearney, R. C. (1993). *State and Local Government*, 2nd ed. Boston: Houghton Mifflin.

Broom, G. F. (1988). Management of growth in conservative communities. *Public Management, 70,* 12.

Burchell, R. W., and Listokin, D. (1980). *The Fiscal Impact Handbook*. New Brunswick, N.J.: Center for Urban Policy Research.

Burlington County N.A.A.C.P. v. Township of Mount Laurel. (1983). 92 N.J. 158, 336 A.2d 390.

Butler, S. R., and Reed, A. B. (eds.). (1990). *New Mexico Capital Improvements Programming Manual*. Albuquerque: University of New Mexico.

Campbell, C., Editor, *Pueblo Chieftan*. (1990, June). Personal interview.

Catanese, A. J. (1988). Planning infrastructure for urban development. In J. M. Stein (ed.), *Public Infrastructure Planning and Management*. Newbury Park, Calif.: Sage Publications, pp. 81–93.

Center for Economic Competitiveness, SRI International. (1987). Solutions brief economic development. *Salt Lake City Tomorrow, Economic Development*. Salt Lake City: Center for Economic Competitiveness.

Cervero, R. (1988). Paying for off-site road improvements through fees, assessments, and negotiations: Lessons from California. *Public Administration Review, 48,* 534–41.

Chandler, W. D. and Mills, N. L. (1989). *An Analysis of the Pueblo Economy*. Unpublished report, University of Southern Colorado.

Charter for the City of Pueblo, Colorado, of 1954. Pueblo, Colorado. (1983).

Charter for the City of Tempe of 1964. Tempe, Arizona. (1984).

Chinitz, B. (1990). Growth management: Good for the town, bad for the nation? *American Planning Association Journal* (Winter):3–8.

City of Clinton v. Cedar Rapids and Missouri River Railroad Co. (1868). 24 Iowa 455, 475.

City of Tempe. (1990). *Annual Budget, City of Tempe, Arizona for the Fiscal Year Beginning July 1, 1990*. Tempe: City of Tempe.

Clack, D., Cowles, W., Redmond, P., and Zirkle, L. (1989). Cover letter to the Momentum 1989 annual report.

Colman, W. G. (1975). *Cities, Suburbs, and States: Governing and Financing Urban America*. New York: Free Press.

Conroy, W. J. (1990). *Challenging the Boundaries of Reform*. Philadelphia: Temple University Press.

Corpus, R., City Manager, Tacoma, Washington. (1990, July 25). Personal interview.

Corsentino, S., City Council Member, Pueblo, Colorado. (1990, July 27). Personal interview.

Davies, L., Ulrich, C., Jr., and Cowan, J. (1979). Arguments in opposition to Measure A. *Ballot Information Regarding Measure A*. City of Modesto, Calif.

Davis, L. J. (1974). Tearing down Boise. *Harper's Magazine* (November):32–38.

DeBruin, L. (1989). Tempe leads survey as least-expensive city. *Mesa Tribune*, Oct. 22, p. A–1.

Decker, J. E. (1987). Management and organizational capacities for responding to growth in Florida's nonmetropolitan counties. *Journal of Urban Affairs*, 9, 47–61.

DePaulis, P. (1991). *State of the City Address*. February, Salt Lake City.

DePaulis, P. (1989). *State of the City Address*. February, Salt Lake City.

DeSantis, V. S. (1990). Profiles of individual cities and counties. In *The Municipal Year Book*. Washington, D.C.: International City Manager's Association, pp. 183–234.

Division of Economic and Community Development. (1990). *Population and Economy*. Salem, Ore.: All America City Folder Pamphlet.

Donovan, T., and Neiman, M. (1992). Community social status, suburban growth, and local government restrictions on residential development. *Urban Affai s Quarterly*, 28, 323–36.

Duncan, J., and Associates. (1990). *Traffic Impact Fee Analysis*. Conducted for Ada County Highway District.

Dye, T. R. (1964). Urban political integration: Conditions associated with annexation in American cities. *Midwest Journal of Political Science*, 8, 430–46.

Eardley, D. (1975). Eardley describes city's choice. *Idaho Statesman*, Oct. 18, pp. 4–5.

Editorial. (1991). The race is over—what does it mean? *Idaho Statesman*, Nov. 6, p. A7.

Eide, G., City Manager; Ingraham J., Assistant City Manager; and Wacker, L., Assistant City Manager, Salem, Oregon. (1990, July 8). Personal interview.

Elazar, D. J. (1984). *American Federalism: A View from the States*, 2nd ed. New York: Harper & Row.

Elkin, S. L. (1992). City and regime. In D. Judd and P. Kantor (eds.), *Enduring Tensions in Urban Politics*. New York: Macmillan, pp. 33–47.

Eugene-Springfield Metropolitan Partnership. (1985). *Eugene/Springfield Oregon Community Profile*.

Faas, R., Director, Washington State University Program for Local Government Education. (1991, March 1). Memo to local government growth strategies forum participants.

Fainstein, S. S., and Fainstein, N. (1983). The ambivalent state: Economic development policy in the U.S. federal system under the Reagan administration. In D. Judd and P. Kantor (eds.), *Enduring Tensions in Urban Politics.* New York: Macmillan, pp. 333–51.

Fery, J. B. (1979). Managing growth for quality of life. Speech delivered to the Greater Boise Chamber of Commerce, Boise, Idaho, Jan. 17.

Fisher, R. C. (1988). *State and Local Public Finance.* Glenview, Ill.: Scott Foresman.

Fleischmann, A. (1986). The politics of annexation: A preliminary assessment of competing paradigms. *Social Science Quarterly, 67,* 128–41.

Florida State Department of Community Affairs. (1989). *Local Government Comprehensive Planning Process.* Unpublished Manuscript.

Fosler, R. S. (1988). The future economic role of local governments. *Public Management, 70,* 3–10.

Foster, Dick. (1989). Pueblo earns rank of comeback city. *Rocky Mountain News,* June 18, p. 1.

Fuhrman, J. Z. (1990). *Boise's Struggle with Foothills Development.* Unpublished manuscript, Boise State University, graduate program in public administration.

Fuhrman, R. (1990). *Attitudes Toward Growth in the Boise Area.* Unpublished manuscript, Boise State University, graduate program in public administration.

Garcia, J. D. (1987). Zoning issues caused biggest 1987 stir in Tempe. *Phoenix Gazette,* Dec. 30, p. A–6.

Geraghty, J., Former County Commissioner, Spokane, Washington. (1990, June 21). Personal interview.

Gerber, S. (1987). Presentation to annexation workshop. Association of Idaho Cities, Boise, Idaho, October.

Gibson, K. (1992). *Annexation Issues in Boise, Idaho.* Unpublished manuscript, Boise State University, graduate program in public administration.

Gleason, M. D. (1990). *Budget Summary 1989–90, City of Eugene, Oregon.* Eugene: City Manger's Office.

Glickfeld, M., and Levine, N. (1992). *Regional Growth . . . Local Reaction: The Enactment and Effects of Local Growth Control and Management Measures in California.* Cambridge, Mass.: Lincoln Institute of Land Policy.

Gold, S. D., and Fabricius, M. A. (1989). *How States Limit City and County Property Taxes and Spending.* Denver: National Conference of State Legislatures.

Gold, S. D., and Ritchie, S. (1992). State policies affecting cities and counties in 1991: Shifting federalism. *Public Budgeting and Finance* (Spring):23–46.

Government Finance Research Center. (1989). *Debt Capacity Study: City of Tempe, Arizona.* Washington, D.C.: Government Finance Research Center.

Gray, B., Director, Washington State University, Spokane, Washington. (1990, June 20). Personal interview.

Haeberle, S. H. (1989). *Planting the Grass Roots: Structuring Citizen Participation.* New York: Praeger Publishers.

Hamburg, Ken. (1992). Boom town. *The Oregonian,* Aug. 9, p. D1.

Hanson, P. J., and Scheffer, M. (1975). *Brief Summary of Public Opinion Concerning Downtown Boise.* Unpublished manuscript, Boise State University, Boise Center for Urban Research, Boise.

Harriman, R., and Shastid, J.G.H. (1979). Rebuttal to argument opposing Measure A. *Ballot Information Regarding Measure A.* City of Modesto, Calif.

Hays, S. P. (1992). The politics of reform in municipal government in the Progressive Era. In H. Hahn and C. Levine (eds.)., *Urban Politics*. New York: Longman, pp. 53–72.

Healy, P. (1974). *The Nation's Cities: Change and Challenges*. New York: Harper and Row.

Herson, L.J.R., and Bolland, J. M. (1990). *The Urban Web: Politics, Policy and Theory*. Chicago: Nelson-Hall Publishers.

Hill, K. Q., and Mladenka, K. R. (1992). *Democratic Governance in American States and Cities*. Pacific Grove: Brooks/Cole Publishing.

Hills Development Co. v. Township of Bernard. (1986). 103 N.J., 1, 510 A.2d 621.

Holli, M. G. (1992). The empty promise of reform. In D. Judd and P. Kantor (eds.), *Enduring Tensions in Urban Politics*. New York: Macmillan, pp. 241–58.

International City Management Association. (1988). Developer financing: Impact fees and negotiated exactions. *Management Information Systems*. Washington, D.C.: International City Management Association.

Johnson, W. C. (1989). *The Politics of Urban Planning*. New York: Paragon House.

Judd, D. R. (1988). *The Politics of American Cities: Private Power and Public Policy*, 3rd ed. Glenview, Ill.: Scott Foresman/Little, Brown College Division.

Judd, D. R., and Kantor, P. (eds.). (1992). *Enduring Tensions in Urban Politics*. New York: Macmillan.

Kane, M., and Sand, P. (1988). *Economic Development: What Works at the Local Level*. Washington, D.C.: National League of Cities.

Kartez, J. D. (1991). *Planning for Cooperation: Local Government Choices*. Occasional paper prepared by the Washington State University's Program for Local Government Education. Pullman, Wash.: Washington State University.

Kelly, E. D. (1988). Zoning. In Frank S. So and Judith Getzels (eds.), *The Practice of Local Government Planning*, 2nd ed. Washington, D.C. International City Management Association, pp. 251–84.

Kempthorne, D. (1990). Idaho's second century: Managing growth and decline. Speech delivered at Boise Conference, Boise, Idaho, Nov. 16.

KPMG Peat Marwick. (1989). *Charges for Services between Funds*. Salt Lake City, Utah: KPMG Peat Marwick.

League of Oregon Cities. (1990). *Oregon's SDC Act*. Briefing paper. Salem: League of Oregon Cities.

Leithe, J. L., and Joseph, J. C. (1990). Financing alternatives. In S. G. Robinson (ed.), *Financing Growth: Who Benefits? Who Pays? And How Much?*. Chicago: Government Finance Research Center, pp. 91–107.

Leithe, J. L., and Montavon, M. (1990). *Impact Fee Programs: A Survey of Design and Administrative Issues*. Government Finance Research Center and David M. Griffith & Associates.

Lemov, P. (1992). The brave new world of public finance. *Governing*, 5, 27–28.

Leutwiler, N. R. (1987). Playing taps for urban growth control: Restricting public utility access to manage growth. *State and Local Government Review* (Winter):8–14.

Lipsky, G. (1990). *Proposed Annual Budget 1990–1991, City of Modesto, California*. Modesto, Calif.: City Manager's Office.

Local Economic Development Act, Idaho. (1988). Chapter 21, Sections 1 to 12.

Logan, J. R., and Rabrenovic, G. (1990). Neighborhood associations: Their issues and their opponents. *Urban Affairs Quarterly, 26,* 68–94.

Logan, J. R., and Zhou, M. (1989). The adoption of growth controls in suburban communities. *Social Science Quarterly, 71,* 118–28.

Lovelace R. (1977). Annexation: A necessary power. *Tennessee Town and City* (October):10–12.

Lowery, D. (1985). Public opinion, fiscal illusion, and tax revolution: The political demise of the property tax. *Public Budgeting and Finance* (Autumn):76–88.

Lowrey, M., Regional Manager, Department of Local Affairs, State of Colorado. (1990, June). Personal interview.

Lupsha, P. A., and Siembieda, W. A. (1977). The poverty of public services in the land of plenty: An analysis and interpretation. In D. C. Perry and A. J. Watkins (eds.), *The Rise of the Sunbelt Cities.* Beverly Hills, Calif.: Sage Publications, pp. 185–86.

Lyman, G. L. (1991). *The City of the Future* (Report No. 10). Boise: Boise Future Foundation.

Mabbutt, R., and Lyman, G. (1985). *Greater Boise's Carrying: The Public Service System.* Boise: Boise Future Foundation, Boise State University.

Mackey, S. (1991). Tax revolts in the West. Speech at Local Government Institute, National Conference of State Legislatures, Boise State University, Nov. 21.

MacManus, S. A. (1985). Mixed electoral systems: The newest reform structure. *National Civil Review, 74,* 484–92.

MacManus, S., and Thomas, R. D. (1979). Expanding the tax base: Does annexation make a difference? *Urban Interest, 1,* 15–28.

Magleby, D. (1988). Taking the initiative: Direct legislation and direct democracy in the 1980's. *PS: Political Science and Politics, 21,* 600–11.

Marando, Vincent L. (1979). City-county consolidation: Reform, regionalism, referenda, and requiem. *Western Political Quarterly, 32* (December):409–421.

Mauldin, F., Director, Public Works, Salem, Oregon. (1990, July 9). Personal interview.

Mauldin, F. (1990). *Street Maintenance Cost of Service Analysis.* Salem, Ore.: Public Works Department.

Mensinger, P., Former Mayor and City Councilor, Modesto, California. (1990, July 19). Personal interview.

Meyer, S., Coordinator, Momentum 1990, Spokane, Washington. (1990, June 20). Personal interview.

Miller, J. C., and Forstall, R. L. (1984). Annexations and corporate changes 1970–79 and 1980–83. In *The Municipal Yearbook.* Washington, D.C.: International City Management Association, pp. 96–101.

Modesto Citizens Advisory Growth Management Act: Measure A. (1979). Ordnance of the City of Modesto, Calif.

Modesto City Planning and Community Development Department. (1990). Briefing materials prepared on behalf of the authors.

Modesto City Resolution No. 89–1132. (1989).

Mollenkopf, J. H. (1983). *The Contested City.* Princeton, N.J.: Princeton University Press.

Molotch, H. (1976). The city as a growth machine. *American Journal of Sociology, 82,* 309–30.

Momentum. (1989). *Annual Report*. Spokane.

Moody, F. (1991). Bridge to the future. *Seattle Weekly*, April 17, pp. 40–49.

Morrison Institute for Public Policy. (1990). *Vision Tempe: Research Reference Report*. Tempe, Ariz.: Arizona State University School of Public Affairs.

Mosher, E. (1982). On behalf of annexation. *Kansas Government Journal, 68*, 47–59.

Mulady, K. (1990). Marketing Boise. *Boise Magazine* (November):29–30.

Munch, J., Director, Planning, Pueblo, Colorado. (1990, June 26). Personal interview.

National Council on Public Works Improvements. (1988). The state of U.S. infrastructure. *Urban Land*, pp. 20–23.

Nelson, A. C. (1988). *Development Impact Fees*. Chicago: American Planning Association.

Neumann, J. (1991). *State Growth Management Legislation: A Comparative Analysis of Legislative Approaches and Administrative Provisions*. Woodrow Wilson School of Public and International Affairs, Center for Domestic and Comparative Policy Studies.

Nevada Assembly Bill 372. (1989).

Nevada Legislative Auditor (1986). *City of Reno—Report on Operations*.

Nicholas, J. C. (1990). *Fiscal Impact Report for Transportation Facilities, City of Reno, Nevada*. Written in conjunction with Icard, Merrill, Cullis, Timm, Furen, and Ginsburg, PA and Omni Means LTD, May 1.

Office of the Mayor and the Bear West Consulting Team. (1991). *Salt Lake City Tomorrow, Phase II*. Salt Lake City: Office of the Mayor.

O'Malley, P., Port Commissioner, Port of Tacoma, Washington. (1990, August 6). Personal interview.

On the road again: Congestion is worse, commutes are better. (1992). *Governing, 5*, 47.

Oregon Department of Transportation. (1990). *Local Road and Street Questionnaire for Fiscal Year Ending June 30, 1988*. Joint publication with the League of Oregon Cities and Association of Oregon Counties.

Oregon House Bill 3224, 65th Legislative Assembly. (1989).

Oregon State Land Conservation and Development Commission. (1985). *Oregon's Statewide Planning Goals 1985*. Unpublished report.

Pace, N., City Council Member, Salt Lake City, Utah. (1991). Personal interview.

Pagano, M. (1988). Fiscal disruptions and city responses to stability, equilibrium, and city capital budgeting. *Urban Affairs Quarterly, 24*, 118–37.

Peirce, N., and Johnson, C. W. (1989). The Peirce report—Puget Sound in the 90's: The challenge of growth, the cost of sprawl, the danger of failing to act. Reprinted from the *Seattle Times*, Oct. 1–8, p. 6.

Peirce, N. R., and Hagstrom, J. (1984). *The Book of American: Inside Fifty States Today*. New York: Warner Books.

Peterson, A. (1992). Land swap spurs grass-roots activism. *Idaho Statesman*, April 12, pp 1, 4A.

Peterson, D. D. (1988). *City Fiscal Conditions in 1988*. Washington, D.C.: National League of Cities.

Peterson, J. E. (1988). Infrastructure financing: Examining the record and considering options. In J. M. Stein (ed.), *Public Infrastructure Planning and Management*. Newbury Park, Calif.: Sage, pp. 94–116.

Peterson, P. E. (1981). *City Limits*. Chicago: University of Chicago Press.

Port of Tacoma. (1989). *Annual Report.* Tacoma, Wash.: Port of Tacoma.

Porter, D. R. (1987). Financing infrastructure with special districts. *Urban Land,* 45, 9–13.

————. (1986). The rights and wrongs of impact fees. *Urban Land,* 46, 16–19.

Price Waterhouse. (1986). *Making the Right Turn: Protecting Investment in Oregon's Roads and Bridges.* A joint publication by the League of Oregon Cities, Association of Oregon Counties, and the Oregon Department of Transportation.

Reed, C. (1990). Pueblo persistently pursues prosperity. *Colorado Business Magazine* (June):49–56.

————. (1987). Pueblo: What's all the talk about? *Colorado Business Magazine* (September):2–5.

Reno City Budget, Fiscal Year 1991. Reno: Reno Finance Department.

Reno Finance Department. (1989). *City of Reno, Nevada Comprehensive Annual Financial Report for the Fiscal Year July 1, 1988 through June 30, 1989.* Reno: Reno Finance Department.

Rhyne, C. S. (1980). *The Law of Local Government Operations.* Washington, D.C.: Law of Local Government Operations Project.

Ross, B. H., Levine, M. A., and Stedman, M. S. (1991). *Urban Politics Power in Metropolitan America,* 4th ed. Itasca, Ill.: Peacock.

Rubin, B. M., and Zorn, C. K. (1985). Sensible state and local economic development. *Public Administration Review,* 45, 333–39.

Salem Public Works Department. (1990). *Street Maintenance Cost of Service Analysis.* Salem, Ore.: Salem Public Works Department.

Salt Lake City Department of Finance. (1989). *Salt Lake City Corporation Comprehensive Annual Financial Report for the Fiscal Year Ended June 30, 1989.* Salt Lake City: Salt Lake City Department of Finance.

Sawers, L., and Tabb, W. K. (eds.). (1984). *Sunbelt/Snowbelt: Urban Development and Regional Restructuring.* New York: Oxford University Press.

Schilling, H., City Manager, Reno, Nevada. (1990). Personal interview.

Sferrazza, P. (1991). Mayor: My record shows accomplishments, slow growth. *Reno Gazette-Journal,* May 5, p. 7B.

Shafroth, F. (1989). The Reagan years and the nation's cities. In *The Municipal Yearbook.* Washington, D.C.: International City Management Association, pp. 115–28.

Shirey, J. F. (1982). National actions affecting local government: Cutbacks and lowered expectations. In *The Municipal Yearbook.* Washington, D.C.: International City Management Association, pp. 47–55.

Simpson, R. (1991). California counties on the fiscal faultline. *California County Spectrum* (Jan./Feb.):S1–S8.

Singell, L. D., and Lillydahl, J. H. (1990). An empirical examination of the effects of impact fees on the housing market. *Land Economics,* 66, 82–92.

Smith, E. (1989). Creating and retaining jobs in Colorado. *Colorado Business Magazine* (February):18–23.

Smith, M. P., Ready, R. L., and Judd, D. R. (1992). Capital flight tax incentives and the marginalization of American states and localities. In D. R. Judd and P. Kantor (eds.), *Enduring Tensions in Urban Politics.* New York: Macmillan, pp. 532–44.

Snell, R. K. (1990). Financing public services for Idaho's second century. Presentation at Idaho's Second Century Symposium, Boise, Idaho, Nov. 16.

South Carolina v. Baker, Treasury Secretary of the U.S. (1988). 108 S.Ct. 1355 (1988).

Southern Burlington County NAACP et al. v. Township of Mount Laurel. (1975). 67 N.J. 151, 336 A.2d 713.

Spratt, T. (1989). Valley's growth has created a few oases. *The Phoenix Gazette*, Aug. 22, p. A–3.

Steel, B. S., Lovrich, N. P., and Soden, D. L. (1989). A comparison of municipal responses to the elimination of federal general revenue sharing in Florida, Michigan, and Washington. *State and Local Government Review* (Fall):106–15.

Stewart, M. Salt Lake County Commissioner. (1990, June). Personal communication.

Stewart, P., Director, Building Industry Association, Modesto, California. (1990). Personal interview.

Stone, C. N. (1992). Urban regimes: A research perspective. In D. R. Judd and P. Kantor (eds.), *Enduring Tensions in Urban Politics*. New York: Macmillan, pp. 48–65.

Swanstrom, T. (1989). Semisovereign cities: The politics of urban development. *Polity, 21*, 83–110.

Tacoma-Pierce County Chamber of Commerce. (1988). *Tacoma-Pierce County.* Tacoma-Pierce County Chamber of Commerce and MARCOA Publishing.

Taussig, D., and Associates. (1990). *Description and Benefits of Mello-Roos Public Improvements Finance Program.* Modesto, Calif.: Finance Department.

Thai, K. V., and Sullivan, D. (1989). Impact of termination of general revenue sharing on New England local government finance. *Public Administration Review, 49*, 61–67.

Thomas, B., Director, Planning, Reno, Nevada. (1990, June). Personal interview.

Thomas, C. S. (ed.). (1991). *Politics and Public Policy in the Contemporary American West.* Albuquerque, N.M.: University of New Mexico Press.

Tseffos, S. (1989). Tempe studies neighborhood advisory board. *Tempe Daily News* March 9, p. B–1.

———. (1988). Tempe trying to revive community by forming neighborhood groups. *Tempe Daily News*, Feb. 10, p. B–1.

U.S. Advisory Commission on Intergovernmental Relations. (1991). *Changing Public Attitudes on Governments and Taxes*. Washington, D.C.: U.S. Government Printing Office.

———. (1987). *Significant Features of Fiscal Federalism*. Washington, D.C.: U.S. Government Printing Office.

———. (1982). *State and Local Roles in the Federal System*. Washington, D.C.: U.S. Government Printing Office.

U.S. Bureau of the Census. (1987). *Government Finances*. Washington, D.C.: U.S. Government Printing Office.

U.S. Conference of Mayors. (1990). *The Federal Budget and the Cities*. Washington, D.C.: U.S. Conference of Mayors.

Urban Land Institute. (1989). *Project Infrastructure Development Handbook*. Washington, D.C.: Urban Land Institute.

Urban Transition Agreement—Streets and Roads. (1987). Agreement between Lane County and Eugene and Springfield cities, Oregon.

Varela, S., City Engineer, Reno, Nevada. (1990, February 27). Personal letter to G. Etcherey.

Voyles, S., Reporter, *Reno Gazette-Journal.* (1991, August 21). Telephone interview.

Wacker, L. (1990). Letter to the editor. *City and State* (July):7.

Warbis, M. (1990). Boise's growth spurt comes with strings attached. *Idaho Statesman* Oct. 7, p. C–5.

Washington House Bill 2929, 51st Legislative session. (1990).

Washington State Growth Management Act ESHB 2929. (1989).

Washington State Growth Management Strategies Committee. (1990). Olympia: Department of Community Development.

Weatherby, J. B. (1978). *Local Self-Government: A Comparative Analysis.* Unpublished doctoral dissertation, University of Idaho, Moscow.

Weber, B. A. (1990). *How Would Measure 5 Affect Oregon's Tax System?* Corvalis, Ore.: Oregon State University Extension Service.

Weisbrod, F., Former City Manager, Pueblo, Colorado. (1990, June). Personal interview.

Welch, S., and Bledsoe, T. (1988). *Urban Reform and Its Consequences.* Chicago: University of Chicago Press.

Western, K. (1988). Leaders vow to revamp selling of state, valley. *The Arizona Republic,* Dec. 21, p. SE–1.

Wheeler, R. H. (1965). Annexation law and annexation success. *Land Economics,* 41, 354–60.

White, A. D. (1992). City affairs are not political. In D. Judd and P. Kantor (eds.), *Enduring Tensions in Urban Politics.* New York: Macmillan, pp. 205–208.

Wilber Smith Associates and Bell-Walker Engineers. (1990). *Local Jurisdiction Highway Needs Assessment Study.* Boise, Idaho: Local Highway Needs Assessment Council.

Wilson, W. (1887). The study of administration. *Political Science Quarterly,* 2:197–222.

Witt, S. L., Steger, M.A.E., Pierce, J. C., and Lovrich, N. P. (1987). Investigating the potential for metropolitan reform: The relative weight of class, attitudinal, ideological and knowledge factors. *Western Governmental Researchers,* 3:57–76.

Wong, K. K. (1988). Economic constraint and political choice in urban policy-making. *American Journal of Political Science,* 32, 1–18.

Wright, D. S. (1988). *Understanding Intergovernmental Relations,* 2nd ed. Monterey, Calif.: Brooks/Cole.

Zerkle, T., City Manager, Tempe, Arizona. (1990). Personal interview.

Zimmerman, J. (1992). *Contemporary American Federalism: The Growth of National Power.* New York: Praeger.

Index

ABOUT THE AUTHORS

JAMES B. WEATHERBY is an associate professor of public administration and political science and Director of the Public Affairs Program at Boise State University. He is a former executive director of the Association of Idaho Cities and was a member of the Board of Directors of the National League of Cities. Dr. Weatherby participates in a wide range of consulting activities, and is President of Weatherby and Associates, a government and public affairs consulting firm in Boise. He is the principal author of the Idaho city and county budget law, and several other laws affecting local government in Idaho. In addition, he has authored and co-authored many additional works on government in Idaho.

STEPHANIE L. WITT is currently an associate professor of political science and public administration at Boise State University. Her articles have appeared in such journals as *Public Administration Review, Western Political Quarterly, American Politics Quarterly,* and the *Review of Public Personnel Administration.* She is the author of *The Pursuit of Race and Gender Equity in American Academe Administration* (Praeger, 1990). She has done training and applied research for various local governments and local government associations in Idaho and Washington state, where she was affiliated with the Division of Governmental Studies and Services at Washington State University.